Library and Information Service

Library materials must be returned on or before the last date stamped or fines will be charged at the current rate. Items can be renewed by telephone, letter or personal call unless required by another borrower. For hours of opening and charges see notices displayed in libraries.

Mr Wrong: Daniella Blechner.

Non Fiction Self Help
Copyright © 2014 by Daniella Blechner

Printed in the United Kingdom
First Printing 2014. Conscious Dreams Publishing. Daniella Blechner.

ISBN

www.daniellablechner.com
www.dingdongitsmrwrong.com

Dedicated to:

My beautiful Gran, Lurline Rebecca Patterson.

You are forever in my heart

About the Author

Daniella Blechner, author of Mr Wrong, is a South London based Writer/Director whose real writing journey began by writing comedy sketches for Youth Project *Phenomenon* '98 featuring Gina Yashere and Richard Blackwood. She has always been a keen writer and penned her first book *All The Happy Animals* and *Lucille and her Great Adventure* at just 8 years old.

At 18 years old she began her career as a performance poet and enjoyed success in bars and clubs in and around London for many years. In 2002 she attended Ravensbourne College where she wrote, produced and directed her first short *Connexions* which was Nominated for Best Screenplay at the BFM Short Film Awards in 2006 and won "Best Open Deck film" when screened at the Cutting East Festival

Daniella won the 2007 Film Fund Award from Lewisham Film Initiative to complete her poetry based short drama *Hair We Are* for the Black History Month Short Film Challenge. *Hair We Are* won the 3rd Best Film at the Images of Black Women Film Festival and has been screened at Chicago International Children's film, Pan African Film Festival, LA and BAMKids Film Festival in New York. It was also screened on The Community Channel. Since writing and directing the film the poem has been included in Nicole Moore's Shangwe *Hair Power, Skin Revolution* anthology.

She is also the author of poetry anthology *7 Shades of Love*, "an eclectic mix of poems written from women and men across the world exploring the Universal theme of Love."

Daniella enjoys examining and reflecting on social issues often laced with a wicked sense of humour. She especially enjoys working with young people and those "at risk" from exclusion in society.

www.daniellablechner.com
www.dingdongitsmrwrong.com
info@daniellablechner.com

Contents

Mr Wrong, Daniella Blechner

Acknowledgements and Thank You's

First and foremost I want to thank my Creator for providing and guiding me through my challenging life experiences and journeys as well as allowing me to see that through every challenge is an opportunity for progression and growth. Without these challenges or 'negative experiences,' I would not be the woman I am today, nor would I be inspired or guided to write this book. For this I am So Grateful!

I would like to thank, with all my heart, all those, both women and men, who contributed and trusted me with their valuable and personal stories. I would like to thank all those who have supported me throughout this journey. You have shown your Love in all sorts of ways, whether it be wise words of advice, attendance at various Mr Wrong nights, encouragement, or simply advertising my page. A special thanks to Candy, who, with her insurmountable patience, showed me how to set up a blog. Another special thanks to Sophia Bailey for guiding me like an angel on my journey to becoming a published author. Thank you too April Reynolds. I am thankful to all!

Thank you to talented animators Amde Ebanks-Anbessa and Jason Lee for awesome illustrations. Thank you to my fantastic editors Sharon Honeywell and E Lee Caleca.

Most importantly, I would like to thank all the Mr Wrongs out there who have made me the woman I am today: a woman who finally Loves herself through the wounds, through the cracks, through the flaws, and through the dark times. Even though it took a while—and many, many of you—I thank you for teaching me that in order to Love, I must first know my own value. I got there!

This book is dedicated to my beautiful Gran Lurline, Rebecca Patterson. She was and is a phenomenal woman. As a woman, she had a hard life, and even though I was blessed to know her for only a short while, I will always remember her Strength, her humour, and her fierce sense of Independence. I strongly believe she was guiding me from the other side to write this book to empower others.

I also dedicate this book to my parents. It's been a hard haul, but I thank you both for everything that you have ever done for me. Life was not easy growing up, and in the midst of being a child, it is near impossible to see your parents as human beings who are simply trying to do their best. I understand now and I love you both immensely! Thank you for helping shape me through hard lessons and through your unconditional Love into the wonderful woman I am today. To you I give thanks! Mum—you taught me that the world was hard. I stood firm in the face of it and I never gave up. You told me I was a writer through your constant submissions of my 'Cat Sat on the Mat' poems to various children's poetry competitions, so immediately I believed. You showed me that as a woman of Black heritage I would have to work ten times harder than others who were not. I worked my butt off and it still hurts! :)

Dad—you have always made me laugh. There are no words to express how much I Love you. You have supported and encouraged me on my journey through writing Mr Wrong. From your funny photo captions on Facebook to your Mr Wrong jokes, I've loved it all. You taught me that there is nothing more powerful than giving without expecting to receive; that the pleasure is in making someone else happy and cared for without wanting anything back at all. Your kindness knows no bounds and has touched me deeply.

Thank you!

love, relationships, and, most importantly, ourselves is vital to understanding why our relationships play out the way they do.

As women, we tend to blame ourselves when our relationships go bad. We think there's something wrong with us, we feel abused and used when the relationship is over, and we feel as though we deserved some explanation or at least the respect of an adult conversation. We've been told "It's not you it's me" or "I just haven't got time for a relationship at the moment" only to find he's dating someone else two days later. Let me be very clear: there is nothing wrong with you. You are worthy and deserving of love, but I've come to realise that we must be right for ourselves before we can offer anything meaningful to another. If you can't or won't do that, you will continue to date Mr Wrong.

I've encountered Mr Wrong many times, and I will guide you through the Mr Wrong manual. I'll set you onto a path of self-discovery that will help you examine your behaviors, reactions, and all those little things that send up red flags in men's eyes. I have not done this alone but with the loving help of women and men all over the world who have contributed their valuable stories. Their tales chronicle everything from light hearted dating disasters to poignant narratives of strength, overcoming adversity and, most importantly, self-discovery.

Mr Wrong has been written with Love and celebrates men who are taking part in affectionate and healthy relationships. Through reading the stories written by men ranging from Ex-Mr Wrongs and confessed Mr Wrongs, to men who have been deeply hurt in a relationship, we are able to gain an insight into the valuable male perspective. What role do women play in creating so called Mr. Wrongs? Can men be solely to blame? How do our expectations and perception of men reflect what we experience?

Mr Wrong offers practical advice, not from just one point of view, but from women all over the world who have shared their experiences and dilemmas with us. Each chapter is designed to inspire, unite, and empower us through interactive quizzes, questionnaires, meditations, and exercises. Mr Wrong allows you to proactively identify Mr Wrong and free yourself from the negative cyclic dance of attracting and being attracted to the wrong men. It will set you on a positive path that frees you to find the perfect Mr Right for You.

Daniella Blechner

Chapter 1:
How Can I spot Mr Wrong?

Identify Mr Wrong

There are many different types of Mr Wrong. Before we start, I want to make it very clear that we are not here to berate or batter Mr Wrong, for we are all on our journey to completion and wholeness. These men still have got a lot to learn about how to have a healthy adult relationship, and we must respect their journey. However, unless you want to keep offering yourselves up as their guinea pigs, then please read on. Here you will be able to identify the many shades of Mr Wrong and perhaps recognise some through experiences of your own. By identifying them, we can recognise them more easily when they present themselves and make the conscious decision to set out for Mr Right instead.

Mr Drifter

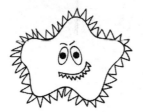

Appearance: Wears a glazed expression and a permanent, yet annoyingly content smile.

Movement: Strolls instead of walks, often nods head and closes his eyes with said content smile glued to his face. On exiting the relationship, his movement is like a piece of driftwood floating in a canal.

Typical Phrase:
"I'll do it in a minute."
"I dunno really."
"How did I get here?!"

Tone of Voice: Often low and quiet, sometimes as if barely speaking at all.

The Drifters fickly float about with no real aim or purpose, flitting from one 'relationship' to another, never quite knowing what they are seeking. They may have lots of different hobbies but none they really stick at or see through; they are jacks-of-all-trades and masters of none. We are attracted to their easy-going nature and laid-back approach—until we realise that "laid back approach" we initially loved is actually aloof on a whole new level and apathy incarnated. These types are prone to drifting into relationships and even marriages not quite knowing how or why they got there. Mr Drifter may have spent time "kipping on sofas" or travelling around "finding himself." Mr Drifters often search for a mother figure to help them realise their dreams—you often fund this dream too. Mr Drifter could spend years in a relationship with you before realising that his dream is not to be a lawyer but to travel to Goa alone. The woman on the receiving end of this may feel deeply betrayed and used. Don't let him drift towards you.

Mr Dreamer

Appearance: Has a refined glow about him, a dashing smile, and hypnotic eyes.

Movement: His movements are delicate, smooth, and precise. His movement on exit differs from Mr Drifter as he moves at the speed of lightning.

Typical Phrase:

"It's you and me all the way, baby."

"It's destiny that you and I met."

"Am I The One?"

Tone of Voice: Silky and enchantingly smooth.

Mr Dreamer has lots of dreams, hopes, and ambitions but nothing written down on paper. Mr Dreamer is often a charming man with a silver tongue and silky words that could convert the greatest cynic into a dedicated disciple. Mr Dreamer lures his woman with fanciful words, flattery, and flamboyant ideas for the future. He will sweep you off your feet and into his cloud. However, sooner or later you're wading through a cloud of dust, wondering where he has gone. It is then that you realise that he has no real intention of settling down, landing that dream job, putting that sparkly ring on your finger, walking you down that aisle, being that fantastic father he never had, or growing old together with you. Did he ever exist, or was he a mere illusion? Leave well alone!

Mr Surfer

Appearance: Wears a happy-go-lucky smile and placid expression.

Movement: Moves quickly and quietly as he darts from one place to the other, swiftly serving and escaping "confrontation" and any perceived trouble.

Typical Phrase

"We can talk about it later, hun."

"We don't need to talk about it right now."

"What do you mean I'm surfing all over your feelings?"

Tone of voice: Quiet, smooth, and calm. Talks as if coaxing a Rottweiler into being amiable.

Mr Surfer is a happy-go-lucky chap who enjoys the company of women but not the reality that being in a relationship brings. Mr Surfer has good intentions but no interest in talking about "feelings" or discussing "issues." He glosses over issues and problems and pretends that they do not exist. As he surfs over the waves, he causes unknown havoc. He may wound his partner with his words or actions but refuses to talk about the repercussions or implications of them. His fear of confrontation or adult discussions causes breakdowns in communication, leaving his other half feeling unheard and unappreciated. She is made to feel like a 'nag' or that her feelings are unimportant while resentment grows deep inside her. This lack of communication and this lack of willingness to take responsibility or to listen withcompassion create a woman who bears, deep inside, the angry Rottweiler Mr Surfer so desperately fears.

Mr Loose Eye

Appearance: Large goggle eyes and gormless expression. Often has his mouth open and has a tendency to dribble.

Movement: Shifty, revolving eyes and a revolving head that can turn a full owl-like 360!

Typical Phrase:

"I'm just looking at her T-shirt!"
"What were you saying?"
"Why are you always accusing me!"

Tone of Voice: Soft and reassuring.

This guy has a revolving eye! Whilst looking you in the eye and telling you you're the best thing since sliced bread, his revolving eye scans the area for a sandwich! This one is easy to spot; it's the darting eyes, snatching furtive looks at any attractive female within his range or the greedy licking of lips, like a kid in a candy store about to dip his hand into the pic 'n' mix trough. Other giveaways are the blatant goggle eyed, dropped jaw, and gormless gawp over your shoulder as he puts his hand on your knee 'reassuringly.' Unless you like to 'share,' he isn't for you. Leave well alone!

Mr Workaholic

Appearance: Small, tired eyes, a tense expression. Rarely smiles. Often has a throbbing vein located at right temple.

Movement: He dashes about like a bolt of lightning attending to his work needs, but slobs about at home.

Typical Phrase:
"I'm working late again, honey."
"In early tomorrow."
"I can't make it. I'm working."

Tone of Voice: Busy, rushed, and tense.

Mr Workaholic, at the start, shows bundles of commitment, responsibility, and reliability; however, pretty soon you find he has no intention of marrying you because he is already married to his job. Usually this man runs about working all the hours God sends, working on one project after another, running around after everyone else to cover up his deep-rooted sense of insecurity and fear of commitment to another **human being.** He is the trusted and dependable employee or boss and commitment-phobic boyfriend, lover, or husband. Even when he is not working, he creates work so that he can avoid any real attachment he may feel towards you. He will always put work first, leaving you at the bottom of the pile wondering why you need to compete with his job. Get rid. Job done!

Mr Serial Liar

Appearance: Not everything that glitters is gold.

Movement: Has a shifty, rat-like nervousness about him. His movements are quick and sharp as he ducks and dives as if dodging a bullet. Often coughs to cover up his lies and scratches his head and nose. Prone to twitching and head turning as he scans the area for trails of his lies.

Typical Phrase:
"Honest, babe."
"It's not you, it's me."
"You're the only one for me."

Tone of Voice: Amateur—changes pitch and tone frequently. Professional—has a slow and steady, reassuring tone.

Mr Serial Liar has a disillusioned existence. In fact, he is so disillusioned that he actually believes his lies. Have you ever had a man, whilst gazing into your eyes, tell you—and actually convince you—that the sky was green? Well, this is he. This man has no qualms about looking you in the eyes and, despite being asked for honesty, repeats a lie over and over again until you are brainwashed into believing it. This man may have multiple girlfriends or may even be married, yet he is able to convince you otherwise, making you out to be 'psycho' or 'mad' for not believing his priceless porkies. These men are duplicitous and deceitful. They want to have their cake and eat it and have you watch them too. These men are the most pitiful as they are afraid to live in reality and to face their own truths. Let sleeping dogs lie and take a hike!

Mr Ex Factor

Appearance: Wears a permanent pained expression as if he's had an unfortunate encounter with a liquor of laxatives.

Movement: Walks slowly with shoulders stooped; he's a broken man trapped in a time warp.

Typical Phrase:

"I'm over her."
"She needs me."
"Me and my ex used to go here."

Tone of Voice: Monotonous and whiny.

This man is not available. He says he wants to move on, yet "Ex" seems to be the only word coming out of his mouth. He constantly compares you to her, speaks to her, plays the concerned ex-boyfriend by helping out with odd jobs, and is there for her. If he's not speaking to her, he talks to you about the pain he went through and is still going through, saying she cheated on him and broke his heart. You are forever feeling second best, and every time he's with you, you can read his mind as he checks his phone to see if she's called. You are so far down on his list of priorities he may even forget to call and to cancel dates. He may make false promises and apologise yet lets you down time and time again. This man is not—I repeat, is not—available. He will never give you the love, security, or attention you deserve because he is still hung up on his ex!

Make a swift ex-it!

Mr Parasite

Appearance: Looks shiny on the outside. Looks are irrelevant as they are deceiving, but if you look close enough, you can see the hooked claws, translucent skin, and sharp fangs beneath his smiling mouth.

Movement: Walks as if he is drained of all energy before feeding yet buzzing with excitement after.

Typical Phrase:
"I'm not blaming you, but it's your fault."
"We need to talk. You've upset me again."
"I don't ask for this drama. You made me do it."

Tone of Voice: Will use any tone of voice necessary to get required 'emotion' across. Often has an accusatory/defensive tone.

Mr Parasite is the most dangerous of all. Sometimes known as 'drainers,' they are usually jealous, possessive, or insecure types who need constant control and power. They'll gain your heart by exposing their emotional side to you in the hope you'll do the same. Before you know it, they've managed to expose your vulnerabilities, doubts, and insecurities so that they can refer to and feed off these later. For example, if you tell them you fear abandonment, they'll threaten to dump you and leave you every time you do something they don't want you to do. Let's say you go to a party with the girls or go on girls' holiday. Their own deep-seated insecurity and fear of abandonment is transferred onto you. Another example could be that, after having told them you have been betrayed before, they go out of their way to make you feel as if they could cheat on you if you displease them. They feed off your insecurities in order for them to grow taller, more powerful. This is, knowingly or not, emotional abuse.

Other parasites could be emotionally needy men who drain your time, energy, and love for fear that you will abandon them. They need constant validation and reassurance and, in doing so, form an unhealthy attachment to you, whereby you become his private supply of all that's positive in his life. These men can also often cause dramas, arguments, and traumas in a desperate attempt to keep the relationship alive by creating urgent and dramatic situations that constantly demand your attention. A man must love himself before he can love another. A man must be secure in himself before he can provide security and equally share love with another. This is a sorry situation, and you will always be his source of energy until you create boundaries and a sense of personal space with this type of man. Better still. Power up and find Mr Right.

These Men Are Unavailable

These men all have one thing in common. They are UNAVAILABLE, whether it is emotionally, mentally, or physically. In light of this, one thing is for sure: if we learn from them and move on, we can grow from them both in strength and in wisdom. We may dwell on the pain and misery they have caused us, but perhaps there is one thing we can thank Mr Wrong for: if we can identify them quickly enough and finally stop blaming and battering ourselves for not getting Mr Wrong to love us, we can recognise exactly what it is we don't want and start focussing on exactly what it is we do!

We are the author of our own destiny, and we make the conscious decisions as to who and what is to enter our lives. Our life is a blank canvass. We are given the tools to paint, create, decorate, erase, remould, and reshape it in any way we see fit. Everything within our unique canvass is there only because we have put or allowed it to be there. If a relationship is making you unhappy, change it. If a man is making you feel unloved or unworthy, remove him from your life. If you feel you've put up with too much for too long, don't beat about the bush, don't spend hours complaining to the girls about how awful your life is. Reshape it, steer it in a different direction, and set out on a path to "Mr Right."

> *"Everything in your life is a reflection of a choice you have made. If you want a different result, make a different choice."*
>
> – unknown

Types of Unhealthy Relationships

There are many different types of relationships. Each relationship is unique and offers different types of rides and journeys. Unfortunately not all relationships are happy and healthy, and here you may be able to identify the different types of unhealthy relationships Mr Wrong has to offer. Whilst no two relationships can ever be the same, there are no doubt patterns and repeated situations that lead to the emergence of repeated outcomes over the course of a relationship. I have often found myself in a relationship thinking, "Erm ... I'm sure I've been here before," and even "Yes. I know what happens next." I have been party to also continuing the negative relationship despite clearly having been presented with the same type of man, the same type of lesson, and the same type of relationship. I have been that woman who has thought, "This time it will be different," or "He's on the verge of changing," only to be presented with the same outcome again and again and again. In a nutshell—an overwhelming sense of pain. I am a headstrong woman, stubborn at times, but after over a decade of dating men who were clearly wrong for me, I've learnt that things will never be different, you can never change a man whilst you are with him, and the only way to escape these types of relationships is to get out. In essence, stop playing the game and get off the ride!

The Roller-coaster

The rollercoaster seems thrilling and exciting whilst standing at the bottom looking up; however, once committed to the ride, you'll find it's full of highs and lows and ups and downs that leave you feeling disorientated, dizzy, and ungrounded. These types of relationships often leave you feeling as though you have lost a sense of yourself through all the drama this relationship has generated. You may feel unsteady, incomplete, and drained once the relationship has ended, wondering why on earth you ever chose to get on. These relationships are often shared with Mr Serial Liar and Mr Parasite who thrive on drama, manipulation, and your energy. Whilst smooth sailing may not be for you, this rollercoaster is neither fun nor fair and therefore should roll out of your life and stay at the funfair!

The Waltzer

This relationship is everything you could wish for in a ride. It's thrilling, exciting, and full of surprises. You are so swept away with the excitement— it's seemingly never ending. Then ... it abruptly stops. While this is great as a ride, it's not a sustainable relationship. These relationships are usually offered by Mr Dreamer, Mr Serial Liar, and Mr Loose Eye. The relationship often comes to an abrupt ending when Mr Dreamer realises that he can no longer sustain his flamboyant façade or indeed fulfil any of the promises he made to you at the beginning of the relationship. Mr Serial Liar will usually offer a longer Waltzer ride as he believes his lies and, at times, is so convincing the ride can be long-term. And Mr Loose Eye? Well, whilst we're still enjoying the ride, he's already jumped off into some other poor, unfortunate soul's bed (and life), leaving you to connect the dots. Mr Wrong has taken you for a ride! Jump off while you can!

Hook-A-Duck

This is where a woman desperately tries to snare her man only to see him slip through her hook time and time again with an unfazed expression glued to his face. After countless attempts, the woman wishes she had a rifle from the cuddly toy stall to shoot that duck down! These types of non-committed relationships are often offered by a typical E.U.M. (Emotionally Unavailable Man, see **Chapter 6**) such as: Mr Dreamer, Mr Drifter, Mr Ex Factor, and Mr Workaholic. They are quite content with offering the absolute minimum whilst the woman does all the work. Of course they wear unfazed expressions. **You** are doing all the work! Their nonchalant attitude feeds and breeds your insecurities and determination to keep hooking and hooking until you eventually blow. As a result, they finally come alive with the inevitable curses of, "psycho," "bunny boiler," and the classic old "neurotic." However, these men remain oblivious that they are the catalyst to this 'neurotic' behaviour. If they had not promised commitment and security from the start and been honest about the type of relationship they wanted instead of drifting or disappearing, she would not have felt the need to cling so tightly. Many women in this type of relationship are left wondering what it was that was so wrong with her that he could not follow through. Ladies, there is nothing 'wrong' with you. Your man just cannot commit. He's unavailable. Let him go and stop fishing!

The Ghost Train

This is a ride where either party is constantly frightened or paranoid about their partner's past. It's a journey where ex-girlfriends, ex-boyfriends and past dramas are resurrected or reincarnated. This relationship is normally formed with Mr Ex Factor or Mr Parasite and other emotional vampires who thrive on drama or past problems to validate their existence. The couple form an unhealthy attachment of insecurity, jealousy, and paranoia.

This ride is full of ghosts, and there are skeletons in closets and unfinished business. A wretched ride!

The 10p Slot Machine

This is a game of push and pull and usually occurs with

Mr Drifter, Mr Dreamer, and Mr Workaholic. Similar to The Hook-A-Duck, one party (usually the woman) is constantly giving, nurturing, and adding to the relationship (synonymous to the coins in the slot) whilst the other ceaselessly plays a game of push and pull, inching closer and closer to the woman only to repeatedly pull away from her. The woman never reaps anything but false hope—a far cry from the love, stability, and commitment she was seeking. This is a painful ride. Stop it now. You deserve better.

Part 1
Other Women's Stories

Chapter 2: First Loves

This book came about partly due to my own past experiences and having listened to others whose experiences sounded all too scarily similar. It's heart breaking to see so many of my thirty-something pals, who I consider to be strong, intelligent, beautiful, vivacious, witty, and independent, repeatedly encountering and sometimes staying with men who clearly do not deserve them or men who simply do not treat them respectfully. So what is it that makes us stay and how do we break away and change the repetitive cycle? Furthermore, how can we identify and shake off Mr Wrong before we get in too deep? In the following chapters you will gain access to the stories and experiences of women who have had a taste of the infamous Mr Wrong.

Start at the Beginning

First, however, we need to start at the beginning. Close your eyes. Think back to your very first experience of romantic love. How did it feel? Do you view this experience as a positive one or negative one? Many people describe their first loves as the "love of their lives," but what does this really mean and how does this impact our future relationships?

Prominent UK socialist Dr Malcolm Brynin, principal research officer at the University of Essex (2009), claims that relationship seekers are better off skipping their first experience of love entirely. He claims that the "euphoria" of first loves can create obstacles and damage in future relationships. First loves are new, exciting adventures where passionate feelings and intimacy are experienced for the first time. Often the intensity of these passionate feelings is difficult to replicate, making it harder to find happiness with a future partner. As The Guardian[1] stated, first loves, "could set unrealistic benchmarks, against which we judge future relationships."

If this is the case, then what about those who have less positive first love experiences?

First loves are no doubt key to our relationship experiences. Quite how they are key is another story, a story that belongs to the individual and individual alone. Some may still carry scars from the past; others may simply look back at it as a fond memory whilst others may measure themselves and their future relationships by the mere memory of their first love. Einstein was an intensely clever man, a genius in fact, yet he himself struggled to explain the equation of first love.

"No, this trick won't work. ... How on earth are you ever going to explain in terms of chemistry and physics so important a biological phenomenon as first love?" -Albert Einstein

---

[1] Cited from Amelia Hill, social affairs correspondent. The Observer, Sunday 18 January 2009

My Very First Love

I was lucky enough to have a positive experience. I was fifteen when I met my first love. We stayed together for three years. We were each other's best friends through tough times, flung together through shared troublesome home lives and teenage angst. We were inseparable. We were Romeo and Juliet and no one was ever going to stop us. I remember my mother, God bless her, being very strict about him coming round. He was only allowed around when we could be supervised, and under no circumstances would any boy be allowed upstairs. And rightly so! In retrospect, I love my mother for that. However, it did mean that I was forever at his house. In the end I was the one who broke his heart. I felt trapped, lost, and uncertain. The Sagittarian in me wanted so desperately to flee and experience the world, to find myself again in a world where I felt I lacked complete direction or control over my life. I had dropped out of college for a second time—or should I say excluded[1]—my mother and father had recently separated, and worst of all, my beloved big sister moved out of the house and went off to University. I felt alone and abandoned. My heart was already broken. Love? I didn't care about love. I was on the verge of a rebellion. I wanted sex, drugs, and R'n'B! I was young, I was wild, and I wasn't having any of this commitment baloney! It is only in hindsight I see just how loving and caring and kind-hearted my first love really was. That it was me who felt I didn't deserve to be loved. And, due to a rapid decline in confidence, I set about becoming my own worst enemy. But that's another story ...

---

1 expelled

The Age of Innocence

What I miss about that age of innocence is the ability to be true to who we are and how we feel. Saying "I love you" came easy. There was no rule as to when or how it should be said or even who should say it first. It simply was a statement of fact. "I love you" did not mean losing face of any sort or that we needed to start planning a wedding or family. It meant exactly that. We loved each other. No games, no drama, no endless thoughts of "expectations" or "stipulations" or "what does this all mean?" Those three simple words came easier in my formative years than it ever has since. I want to hold onto that innocence, that wanton abandon, and surrender to raw emotion without fear of rejection or anxiety that it may be "too soon."

When we are young, we tend to grab onto life with both hands, say what we see, and express how we feel without fear of 'messing it up' or 'not getting it right.' As we get older, however, our minds store negative experiences, our minds tell us we need to protect ourselves from being hurt, our minds form thought patterns that create walls around our hearts by trying to rationalise and dilute our feelings. Our minds become plagued with thoughts such as, "I'm not making that mistake again," "I'm not going to tell him how I feel because last time ....," or "I'm going to play it cool this time because ...." Many a relationship has failed because one or both parties have not been honest about their emotions. Too often we place too much emphasis on past experiences and that prevents us from moving forwards into happiness. This applies to both men and women. We need to gain a little bit of that balance back. This does not mean being foolish and gushing all over the next man or woman we take a liking to, but opening up our hearts to new experiences and people, to not let the past dictate how we act, and to remain true and honest about our feelings. Feelings are there to be expressed not imprisoned. When a child smiles or laughs, it means they are happy. When a child cries, it means they are unhappy or that their needs are not being met. When a child hugs, cuddles, or says, "I love you," it comes as easy as the sun shines. There is a lot we can learn from children.

Young Love

Jim and I were seeing each other for ten years on and off, when I was 16 and he was 17. I had always liked him, and we had been childhood friends for a very long time. We lived in a small village in Suffolk, and I was the "girl from home." When I was 19, I went off to go to University in London. Although we remained close and despite ringing each other once a week, he said that he didn't want to commit and wanted me to "enjoy my first year of Uni." However, four months into Uni, his brother came to visit me and told me that Jim was going out with Esmeralda, a much hotter, cooler girl from school. I had to totally accept that if I wanted to keep my friendship with him. However, I wondered why he wasn't able to go out with me four months before, yet he was able to go out with "the hot girl from school," which felt like a betrayal.

I felt that perhaps to him I would always be the "girl from home who would always be there." Heartbroken, I moved on with my life. Nine months later and finally armed with a boyfriend, Jim tried to kiss me on an evening out back home. I distinctly remember my friend at the time stopping this from happening although in my heart I still loved him. Jim apologised and understood that I had moved on. However, a few months later my current boyfriend ended it all, and I went travelling for a year. When I came back, Jim and I began "seeing each other again." We'd shared a kiss here and there and began to get quite close again. I remember sitting with him just after a passionate embrace and tender kiss and him saying, "Let's do this. We should try it. Let's have a relationship. This time I'm serious. It was always meant to be us two."

The next day, I was full of excitement and happiness. I was giving it a go! I'd taken the leap between friends and a full-on relationship with someone I had loved for so long. I remember telling my friends at the time that I was giving it a go with Jim and that I was finally going to take the plunge. As I was strolling along the streets of Soho with them, the sun beating down on me, I heard someone shout my name. "Andrea!!" As I turned round, lo and behold there was Jim, sitting outside a café on a date!! The embarrassment still nips me to this very day, and I still remember the look on my friends' faces as I had to explain that the guy shouting my name was indeed Jim.

Years later he asked me to marry him. I laughed, as I thought he was joking, and in a merry state I ended up snogging his friend. As I popped to the little girl's room, I came back to find them in a full-on fight. I hadn't realised that Jim was deadly serious and that I'd broken his heart as he'd broken mine years back. It's been a good six years and we haven't spoken since. What I have learnt from this is that even though this story seems, and is, in retrospect, laughable, the rejection I felt after seeing Jim on his date with such a pretty girl was the beginnings of my insecurity when it came to men and that my rejection of Jim may well have had the same effect. When we're young and dumb, we react out of immaturity but don't quite realise the effects of our actions.

Andrea, 30, Suffolk, England

My Dreamer is Not My Superman

I met my first love at a theme park. I was a late starter at 19 and hadn't had a 'proper' boyfriend before. He oozed confidence and charm, and I was swept away with the magic of it all. He was out with his friend, and I was out with mine, and we teamed up to go on the most adventurous and scariest rides—with me, of course, sitting next to him, gripping onto his arm. Little did I know this would be a metaphor for our relationship.

The next five months were a whirlwind. He was pretty full on and wanted to get things moving fast. He told me he loved me into our third week of our relationship, and we were inseparable. He would ring me all the time and want to know where I was. I thought this was quite sweet, and I just got caught up with the intensity. He told me he wanted to marry me into our third month and even spoke about weddings and children. I hadn't experienced anything else so had nothing to compare it to. He was so handsome and full of charm I couldn't resist getting swept away in the fantasy. My mother, however, was wary, and she told me to slow down. She also said that I did way too much for him. I lent him money, I helped him apply for jobs, and I even leant him my car. He would repay me with flowers and chocolates. He was my knight in shining armour.

Then one day, just out of the blue, my Mr Dreamer vanished. My mother said she had never trusted him. She could never understand why he would need to keep borrowing money when he spent most of his nights out raving. I didn't see it though. Rather than accept it for what it was, I spent months wondering where my Prince Charming went. My dad left when I was 12 years old, and this was the beginning of a great insecurity for me. I would time and time seek that whirlwind type of relationship I'd experienced as my first love with Mr Dreamer and end up getting hurt when they disappeared. I experienced five Mr Dreamers and five painful heartbreaks over the course of four years. All of them, "Waltzer ride relationships." I felt that there was something wrong with me—something that needed to be fixed. If my dad felt I deserved abandoning, surely the men I dated would see it too. I began to expect it.

It wasn't till seven years later I met Clark. Clark was not my usual type. He was quite geeky, a little awkward, and definitely not the most fashionable man. He was my Clark Kent, but I just hadn't realised! We became good friends. I didn't see him as a potential boyfriend at first—this is probably why I felt so comfortable with him. We'd laugh at the same silly things, and he had the most wicked sense of humour. We both used to wait tables, and he used to mock commentate the conversations happening on each table. "Table Number 3—'Are you checking the waiters out?' 'No, I'm not, but you've got to admit they're pretty cute. By the way, are we going Dutch?'"

He was exactly who he said he was on the tin. He eventually asked me out, doing one of his famous commentaries: "Man on Table 2 says to his wife, 'Now there's a cute couple if ever I saw one. Why doesn't that silly, awkward waiter ask out the gorgeous girl before she gets snapped up?'"

That was five years ago and we've been happily married ever since. I learnt from my experience that there are wolves in sheep's clothing. I found my Mr Right by making the conscious decision to embrace someone different. All that glitters is not always gold; sometimes the real gold is the quiet, geeky, awkward guy who doesn't shower you with hearts and flowers or compliments and charm but takes time to know you and earns your trust and respect. I have met the love of my life and the man of my dreams. Looking back, I can't believe I allowed Mr Dreamer to reel me into his fantasies and that

I allowed my self-esteem to plummet so low I believed I deserved it. My first loves, although hurt, eventually taught me my value.

Holly, 29, Birmingham, England

Going to Goa

I met Michael at a gig. He was a long haired musician with a cheeky smile. He was magnetic and I knew instantly that I wanted him. He and I got together almost straight away. He was a bit flaky and cancelled our first few dates but when we got together it was great. I was 20 at the time and he was a little older, at 24.

We moved in together when I was 21 but as Michael didn't have a steady job I paid most of the rent and bills. He was constantly searching for work playing gigs and never seemed able to hold down a standard job. He worked in record shops, supermarkets, cafes, you name it, but his laid back approach meant that he was always late and somehow always ended up fired or walking out. Things were getting hard. I wanted to go to university but I was struggling with the rent and it became hard shouldering his share as well. I think at one point I was even paying his telephone bill!

My father absolutely hated him and my mother wasn't keen either. She said he was more like a child than a man and that I was his mother. He was so gentle and kind spirited with such amazing talent that I was simply enamoured by him. I wanted him to be successful so much that I paid money from my savings to help him achieve his dream of going to music school. He did this and he made many close friends and started a band. He began gigging more and even though he came home to me every night, I felt side-lined. I didn't go to university in the end and our relationship drifted on for

6 more years. Throughout this time I watched many of my friends settle down and get engaged and wondered if this would ever be us.

When I finally bought up marriage and children he didn't seem adverse to it but never made steps to make more of a commitment. It began to anger me that he would seem to have money to get drunk and go to gigs but was still unable to fully pay his share of the rent, however we drifted on like this for another five months.

One day I remember coming home and he was sitting there on the sofa with his guitar. He was playing me a song when he suddenly stopped and said, "Babe, I've decided I'm going to Goa. I need to find myself. I can't carry on like this. It's not anything to do with you. I just have to go."

My heart broke into tiny pieces and I will never forget how I felt. So he had enough money to go to Goa but after all these years could not pay the rent or bills? It was as if someone had put a dagger right through my heart. I was a mug. I had been a mother all these years to a drifter who didn't know what he wanted out of life. I'd provided the security and stability and got nothing in return. I have no one to blame but myself but what I have learnt from this experience is that I will never again allow myself to be used as someone else's security mat. I now put myself first and voice my needs. I should never have allowed this to have gone on for so long.

I'm lucky as, six years later, I am now engaged to a wonderful man who makes sure that I am secure and happy and I know I never have to worry as we always talk about our hopes and dreams for the future together as a couple.

Jo, 32, Perth, Australia

Mr Surfer

I met Joe when I was only 17. He was my first love. He was four years my senior. Things progressed quite quickly, and we moved in together when I was 19. He told me he loved me almost immediately, and I felt so special. However, Joe was always busy. He worked as a plasterer and was always away from home doing odd jobs. He was, on the surface, a happy-go-lucky, cheeky chappy. He hated anyone complaining and wouldn't hear about any kind of problems or issues in my life at all. He would just brush them off with, "Don't stress, babe," "You worry too much," or his all-time favourite, "Stop moaning."

Soon after we moved in together, I discovered texts from random girls on his phone. He would wave it away when I questioned him and turn the tables as though I was in the wrong for snooping. I felt bad for snooping, but he had been answering his phone and walking out of the room secretly and was receiving phone calls late at night. I'd become suspicious. This carried on for the next year. Whenever I confronted him, he'd just laugh it off as if I was crazy. He was so laid-back, cool, calm, and collected. He coolly told me I was paranoid and neurotic to the point where I thought I was going crazy. The texts were very suggestive, but he would say it was friendly banter and carry on. He told me if I continued to be paranoid, he would leave. It felt like my feelings didn't matter. I had no idea he was doing this to others too. I learnt to suppress my feelings and tread on eggshells. I learnt to suppress my anger too and stop questioning for fear I'd be labelled "neurotic" or a "bunny boiler." I began to think that somehow his feelings and his life were superior to mine. It's sad now when I look at it. He was the classic Mr Surfer- a cheating one.

He continued to gloss over his lies and my insecurities with the cool confidence of a surfer, and I gradually became more introverted.

I became so introverted I would have an internal dialogue with myself, imagining what I would say when I eventually caught him and how I would say it. I drove myself insane.

Eventually, one day I did catch the cheating scumbag in bed with another woman in our home.

Now, I was a quiet and peaceful girl who would do anything to keep the peace, but on this occasion, I completely lost it. I was like a wild animal. A Rottweiler gone mad. I'd proved him right. I was neurotic!

I dumped him and sunk into depression for months. I flitted from one relationship to another. I'd turned from a happy-go-lucky girl to someone who was now always on guard and looking for signs of cheating. I would never be able to communicate properly with my partner; instead I'd sulk like a child or become passive-aggressive by freezing them out for days. I'd learnt to stuff my emotions down. I found myself acting erratic and become emotionally distant and paranoid. I would bottle so much up. I'd eventually flip out and release my anger like the Rottweiler unleashed that day I'd caught my first love cheating. I would accuse them of cheating and all sorts of things. Men simply would not put up with me, and I endured heartbreak after heartbreak for five years. Until I met Dan.

Dan taught me how to talk again. He was so tender and loving and so open. He made me feel like it was safe to communicate, to express my feelings without fear of ridicule or anger. I began to feel myself again. The sulking stopped, as did the deathly silences and outbursts of anger. I've learnt that communication is the key to a healthy relationship. I am now happily engaged to Dan for seven months and can't wait to start my new life with him. I love Dan and thank him for bringing my sanity back and restoring me to a world of communication.

I would say to women who are with men who don't listen to or respect their feelings to remember that your feelings are valid. You do not have to put up with cheating or men lying to you. If you feel something is wrong, speak up. If they continue to wave you away and be dishonest, get out. Don't let them intimidate you. You deserve so much more!

Jackie, 31, Milton Keynes, England

The Lover: You're Nobody till Somebody Loves You

I've missed the train, boat, and plane to love on many occasions, and yet I'm still full of wonder (and a little admiration) at the knowledge of those well-matched couples who have stayed together through thick and thin, through sickness and health, unto death us do part.

It's no good. I have to own up and accept that relationships are my weak point and—at the ripe age of 59 as I write this—it is still better to have loved and lost than never to have loved at all. I know it's a cliché, but I do believe in love, in romance, and especially in passion, which stirs up your feelings to an intensity that's almost too great to bear.

I've had my fair share of relationships, starting with a lot of 'dating' in my late teens. If I was a fly on the wall during those times, I'd wonder at the short-lived 'relationships' with young men that I'd end, often quite abruptly, after a matter of a few weeks. Why? I was ruthless. Going out on a couple dates with potential boyfriends, I would soon see the wood for the trees and stop them in their tracks. It was over before it began, much to the dismay of the dismissed 'boyfriend'. These young men were mostly interested in having fun in the name of sex—no surprise there. But I wasn't interested. Often, (I guess) these 'potential' boyfriends would feel so rejected, dejected even, that they would lie to their men friends and say we'd actually had sex. That seemed the only way they would save face.

Oblivious, I would not give up since I believed this dating game was a process of elimination and one day I'd meet 'Mr Right' and he would want me, warts and all, rather than want my body first and foremost. All of this research (and dating) was, of course, doomed since most young men are thinking with their penises. So my search became too much, as my 'reputation' of yo-yoing in and out of dating became a thing to watch, even by the nicest of young men who would ask probing questions about how many men I'd had sex with. My problem, dilemma even, was that I was in search of love, of romance, and ideally a steady boyfriend, one whom I could laugh with, cry with, chat rubbish with, and with no pressure to give up the goods.

I tried, believe me, I really did. I'd try to reason on the sex issue and say I wasn't ready—yet—offering a glimmer of hope and that I needed to 'get to know' him first. He would counter-reason and say he needed, wanted, to express his 'love' for me; he needed to get closer. The plot thickened, and if he stared intently at me with a deprived look as a puppy begs for more cookies, I'd give him a reassuring kiss and hug and say, 'Soon, soon, we'll explore that side of the relationship.' Often, the response would then be a lengthy silence while he wallowed in self-pity and became cool and aloof. I often lost interest at this stage.

I wasn't stupid; I wasn't going to get caught out like a few of my girlfriends who, at the age of 16, were having babies (yes, in the plural). I remember going to visit one friend and her newborn baby, and the sight of all that baby-mother interaction, particularly witnessing her changing her baby's nappy, was impossible for me to relate to. It was as if our social friendship ended right then and there. That was it—I didn't see her for ages.

My search for love and romance continued, and at the age of 17, something remarkable happened. I met a young man, aged 24, at a night club in Northampton called The West Indian Club. I was living in Wellingborough at the time, a small town ten miles from Northampton. The Wellingborough black girls I knew then used to think the Northampton black boys were a bit of a catch—I couldn't think why. It was a romantic notion, although I have to admit that when the Northampton boys did pay us a visit at a West Indian Dance event in Wellingborough, they did bring some excitement, much to the annoyance of the local boys, so maybe that was it. I remember when I dated a really attractive man whom I'd met in London and had invited up to stay in Wellingborough for the weekend, I was interrogated by my girlfriends as we chatted in the loo between partying. They wanted to find out, "Where did you meet a guy like that?" Now, this I totally understood; a guy from London city was something to talk about. But the Northampton boys versus the Wellingborough boys—I didn't get it—then.

Anyway, my encounter with Tony took me by surprise as I'd never seen such a gorgeous-looking man before. He was perfectly built, firm, fit, and tall (most important as I'm 5' 7" myself), and his body aroma was intoxicating yet soothing. He was dressed casual but smart and wore a hat—a trilby I think. He asked me for a dance, and we danced like a dream (another important factor as I loved to dance), and he wouldn't let me go. It's always nice to be wanted. He asked me a few questions, like my name, where I lived, my age (to which he responded that I hadn't started to live life yet), and so on, and for once it didn't feel like a chat-up script.

Tony's dark mahogany skin was like satin and beautiful to touch. My soft, sepia-brown, sensitive skin, and his smooth dark complexion complemented each other; the contrast was in perfect harmony. Our hot cheeks were joined and the whole of my body merged with his; our dance movements were subtle yet sensuous and exciting. Our bodies were snug and fit like a glove. It was as if only we mattered in that hot, dark, crowded night club atmosphere full of deep bass vibrations and quality acoustics, which just compounded and accentuated the 'romantic' scenario. A flame was simmering and warming up nicely.

There I was, dancing close in a cosy corner, reggae rhythms enveloping me, darkness surrounding us except for the ray of light coming from the DJ's corner space. Tony's whisperings of sweet nothings were purring with delight in my ear, which made me quiver and shiver. When he kissed me, my heart surely did skip a beat; it was an electric moment and I knew then that I was under his spell.

There was no doubt in my mind that Tony was heaven sent. I thanked God for sending him to me. We danced the night away. During all of this 'bliss', time stood still. I was in a trance, oblivious to where and my friends were. I knew nothing about this man. He wasn't even an acquaintance. Nothing else mattered but us being close, and we were caught up in the moment.

Tony and I, our minds weren't in sync. I thought that, like our bodies, our minds were also in harmony. However, Tony's agenda was to have sex with me, and my agenda was to enjoy the exhilaration of being in his arms. I could have danced with him all night, and I would have been satisfied with just kissing, just caressing. In my mind I was thinking that this was such a beautiful way to start a relationship; Tony could definitely be my boyfriend, and once I'd got to know him I could visualise a good relationship developing. I was, of course, playing Russian roulette. Both of us felt passionate on that dance floor, and I just didn't want the night to end. I wanted to be with him.

But the fact is that Tony was probably as disappointed as I was with our sexual encounter later that evening, or should I say the early hours of the next morning. It wasn't until we were getting even more passionate in his bedroom that I announced my virgin status. His face looked a mixture of surprise and disbelief and hidden was the realisation that the sex wasn't going to flow. It was going to be more like a fumble than a night of passion.

What I wasn't prepared for was being a one-night stand. Need I say more? Being a virgin on this occasion wasn't necessarily a good thing either since I remember us having sex and that it was unlike anything I had thought possible. My memory of the sex is vague; it was a strange experience and didn't feel sexy at all; it felt rather clinical and distant. I had an abstract awareness of the deed that had been done, but gone was any romance. And it hurt. I didn't know what to think or feel, even though when we met, danced, and kissed earlier, it felt so good.

After having sex for the first time, it was like the end rather than the beginning. First times are always a bit risky, tricky. There are such a lot of unwritten codes to unfold, and all of this is happening in such a short space of time. I was naïve, but hey, I was only 17 at the time. I thought Tony wanted to see me again. When I left, he asked me out on a date the following week. I took myself off to meet up with him again, but Tony stood me up and I was left feeling abandoned, confused, and hurt. I felt disillusioned and slowly had to come to terms with the fact that the whole evening of bliss with Tony was now a thing of the past. I was left with finding my way out of the maze of hurt and disappointment for a while.

This was the start of my sex life, the start of my life's journey of sexual discovery.

Two years later, when I was 19, our paths crossed again, and my one-night stand with Tony extended to two. This time it was a mutual agenda mixed with my desire to express how I'd matured sexually and was somehow more 'worthy', but by then Tony had a girlfriend and a baby ....

Nicole Moore, 59, London, England

The Interactive First Love Quiz

Try the Interactive First Love Quiz. Sometimes it is good to reflect on our past relationships in order to recognise any reoccurring patterns or changes we have made to our lives. Sometimes we need to get perspective to see how far we've come, to reflect upon our own journeys. The quiz below will help you to identify any reoccurring themes/patterns/attractions that may be helping you forward or perhaps holding you back. Try to answer the questions as honestly as you can and see what conclusions you draw. Enjoy!

First Love to Last Love Quiz

How old were you when you first met your first love?	How old are you now?
Where did you meet your first love?	Where did you meet your first/current love?
What did you look for in a man?	What do you look for in a man now?
What first attracted you to your first love?	What first attracted you to your last/current love?
What was your happiest memory together?	What was/are your happiest memory with your last/current partner?
What were your dreams/goals and ambitions when you were with your first love? Career? Love life?	What are your dreams/goals and ambitions now?

What were the positive qualities of your first love?	What are the positive qualities in your last/current partner?
What were the negative/ unattractive qualities in your first love?	What were/are the negative/ unattractive qualities in your last/current love?
What would your first love say your positive qualities were?	What would your last/current love say your positive qualities were?
What would your first love say your negative/unattractive qualities were?	What would your last/current love say your negative/ unattractive qualities were?
If you argued, what did you argue about?	If you argue/d, what did you argue about?

On a scale of 1-10, how confident were you?	On a scale of 1-10, how confident were/are you?
How did you feel about yourself then?	How do you feel about yourself in your last relationship/now?
What were the negative aspects of your relationship?	What were/are the negative aspects of your relationship?
What were the positive aspects of your relationship?	What are the positive aspects of your relationship?
If you could change anything in your relationship, what would you change?	If you could change anything in your relationship, what would you change?

What has changed?

_____

_____

What's stayed the same?

_____

_____

What would you like to change?

_____

_____

How are you going to change it?

_____

_____

Chapter 3: Dating Disasters and Red Flags

Dating is essential when getting to know someone. Always take a dip with someone before diving in. Dating gives you the opportunity to really get to know the man you may end up in a relationship with. Through conversation and experiencing shared interests you can observe and learn different aspects of your date's personality, etiquette, and social skills in different settings.

For example, after many interesting and thoughtful phone conversations with a man I'd met online, we finally met up on a date. Within minutes of our arrival at the restaurant, he was barking orders at the poor waitress as if she were a lap dog and he was an Army officer. Just as I know I would make a terrible lap dog, I knew at once he was not suited to me. I didn't like his style, so I gave him his marching orders. Respect is a right and not something that should be earned, and if he's talking to a waitress in this way, it tells me a lot about what he could be like in a relationship: demanding, expectant, disrespectful, and downright rude. I wanted a man who was respectful, polite, kind-hearted and easy-going. If I had not gone on a date with him, I would never have got to see how he interacted with members of the public.

Before you go on a date, think about the positive traits you need and want in a man and beware of the red flags and early warnings signs that tell us that this man may not be a match for you. It's far better to discover this early on in 'date phase' than after jumping in head first and spending the entire two months cosying up and watching DVDs at his place. This chapter details stories and experiences of women who have been on the receiving end of a dating disaster but been fortunate enough to have a lucky escape!

Whilst expecting our dates to be fantastic, we must also ensure we are on point too. This is the part of the book where I share one of my most embarrassing moments (a long, long time ago, I may add). My dating disaster is as follows:

I met a guy on New Year's Eve, and we had a great time dancing all night. We were having so much fun we hardly got to talk. We talked online for months until we finally met up for a drink in a local bar in South East London. We were having a jolly old chat when I distinctly remember him saying that he loved how I was so dynamic and energetic. At this point, I noticed that there were tables and chairs on the roof above us. (I think it was part of an art display.) When he went to the toilet, I thought it was a great idea to climb up the ladder and surprise him—show him just how dynamic and spontaneous I was! However, a little while later I heard the bouncer come outside, scan the area, and lock the door. I was locked outside! I saw my date glance through the window of the door to find that the door was locked. Luckily, he saw me waving frantically at him to get his attention. He disappeared off to get the bouncer.

To this day I can distinctly remember having to walk backwards down the ladder with the bouncer loudly advising my date in a thick Nigerian accent, "You better watch for this one. She's crazy! Why did she climb up the ladder?"

Whilst we went on a few more dates after that, it never developed into anything serious. We remained friends, and we learnt a lot from each other; however, something tells me I wasn't taken seriously after that!

What I've learnt about the dating process is that it is good to enjoy yourself, but if you are serious about wanting to pursue a relationship with that person, think how you might want to present yourself. You probably don't want a bouncer telling your potential boyfriend that you are "possessed by crazy fairies" before you have cemented anything real.

Dinner Date

Having been single for a few months, I finally decided to accept a date from a work colleague, totally disregarding the old adage about not dipping your pen into the office ink. I just thought that I might as well live a little. He was cute and had a good personality, and we had been flirting, so why not? He promised to take me to an exquisite restaurant with gourmet food and top-notch service.

On the night of the date, he picked me up in his car and even opened the door for me. He was even wittier and funnier than usual and was saying all the right things and being extremely complimentary. How could this not be the beginning of a great night?

The restaurant, however, had no ambience, the service was flat, and the food was some of the worst I had tasted. Gelatinous risotto and dry pheasant do not do it for me. Furthermore, it seemed that Percy Pepper and Suzy Salt were on a vacation! That was my take; however, my dining companion still thought that this place was the best thing since sliced bread. To cap it all off, the bill was grossly overpriced, but my date put his hand in immediately and said that he had asked me out, so he would pay.

He drove me home, and as we parked outside my house, I thanked him for the good time, and he then leaned in for a kiss. I instantly recoiled and explained that I liked him but only as a friend. He seemed to understand and didn't seem offended ....

The next week at work I came in and logged into my computer and waited for my emails to update. Among the new emails I saw one from my date. I clicked on it, expecting a cheery good morning laced with some witty repartee. Instead, I got a short, sharp monosyllabic request for me to pay for half the bill since I had told him that we wouldn't be anything more than "friends". This is the reason I always insist on splitting the bill!

Ms Won't Date a Co-Worker Again! 28, London, England

Milton the Mortician

Last night I went on a blind date with a man named Milton at a bar called The Magician in the Lower East Side. I arrived first and was dismayed to find that there were, in fact, no magicians at The Magician. There were a lot of gay men and balloons, however.

As I sat and waited at the bar, an old man with wooden teeth and a partially healed head wound sat as close to me as he could. "You're good-looking. I can tell. ... Who's keeping you warm tonight? ... You're not waiting until marriage are you?" were just a few of his disturbing attempts to lure me.

At last, Milton arrived. Although I had hoped someone named Milton would be wearing slacks, a top hat, and a monocle, he was actually wearing jeans and a purple shirt. We moved to a table, and I realized that I had set up a date with an undertaker. Not really—I think he worked for Fox News or something—but his slow, deep voice and lack of any facial expression whatsoever made me wonder if he delivered eulogies in his free time.

We stayed at The Magician for exactly one drink before he suggested we go to a goth bar down the street. Everyone there was dressed in their best gothic attire, and it was incredibly dark and smoky. I struggled to keep the conversation going as Milton the Mortician stared so hard at the candle on the table; I wondered if he was trying to will the flame out with his soul.

When the girl sitting at the table to my right threw up all over the floor, Milton suggested we head to a bar in Brooklyn instead. His exact words were, "I'm feeling good. Are you good, kid?" Umm, yes? He was paying for a cab, so naturally I found this suggestion to be to my advantage.

The third location of the evening was a metal bar in South Williamsburg. It was covered in all sorts of music/death paraphernalia and had a giant wheel you could spin to win gross things to drink. I spun and got a Guinness. Gross. I pondered why Milton kept prolonging the evening if he didn't have anything to say. He was cute: tall, dark, broad features ... but had strange matter in his hair and something on his nostril that had been bugging me since the magic bar. I studied his stoic expression and silent stare and decided that maybe I was wrong about him being a mortician. He was most likely a zombie.

As my beer came to an end, he still hadn't eaten my brains, so I got up to use the restroom. When I returned to the table, I saw that he was on his OKCupid app, checking out available girls in the area. OKCupid has a feature called "Locals" where, if you turn it on, it shows your general location to other people looking to meet for a quick-fix in your proximity. The feature freaks me out and reminds me of Grindr, so I always keep mine off. Perusing for another girl to meet up with while you're still out with the first one? That's a no-no.

I started to put on my coat, and he came back to life for a second, saying, "You want to know why I chose you to go out with?" Well, you make it sound like you are either shopping for the best deal on cold cuts at your local deli or that I am about to be your next victim in a long line of serial slayings ... but why, pray tell, was I chosen? "Because you look exactly like Aubrey Plaza." Apparently The Mortician was a Parks and Recreation fan. The only reason I know about this actress is because I looked her up after someone mistook me for her and asked for my autograph at a bagel store in Boston. Hey, I'll take it. ... She's cute, right? I told Milton he looked like Adam Beach, who, for those of you who don't know Law and Order SVU, was the worst actor ever to star on that show. He really did look a lot like him though. If Adam Beach was a zombie.

Outside, we gave each other a dry good-bye, and he took off down the street, presumably to go meet another OKCupid girl and stare silently at inanimate objects for a couple more hours.

Ahhh, another date where I leave with my life.

Langley Denton, 28, New York City, USA

Judgemental Jonah

Have you ever wondered who the most negative man in all of New York City is? What does he do? Where does he live? Well, your search is over because I went on a date with him on Wednesday night. He works in the West Village and lives in Astoria. ... We'll call him "Jonah."

I try not to meet up with anyone from OKCupid who appears to be super serious because I'm not, so it is usually a serious waste of my time. Under "You Should Message Me If" I even put "You don't take yourself seriously!" (among other things). Unfortunately, the serious guys must not think they're serious because my disclaimer has not always proven to work very well.

Jonah had originally messaged me while he was in Washington, DC, on a business trip. I told him to bring me back a patriotic key chain, and his response was to sketch various keychain possibilities on Post-it notes, stick them on his face, and send me pictures of this. I thought "Hey, surely this guy must have a sense of humor about himself if he puts Post-its on his face." Wrong. The red flags I chose to ignore on his profile were: Diet: "Strictly vegetarian," Pets: "Doesn't like dogs and doesn't like cats," I want my next relationship to last: "For the rest of my life." He additionally noted that he wasn't looking for a "flimsy relationship comparable to the durability of IKEA furniture." I also noticed that he had answered one of the questions indicating that he would be interested in having sex with a man, which didn't really seem to fit the rest of his profile.

We met at Art Bar after I got off work. Apparently, on his way into the bar, he accidentally introduced himself to another girl he thought was me who was also waiting to meet someone from OKCupid. The girl was about four inches shorter than I, curvy, with pitch-black hair, bangs, and a pair of white arms that were covered in tattoos. After they sorted out the mix-up, the girl found her date and Jonah found me. He had fluffy, dirty-blonde hair and looked much older in person than he did online.

He sat down at the bar and positioned himself so that he could stare at the other girl for the next hour. Although I attempted to have a conversation with him, he constantly glanced over at their table and kept interrupting me to give updates on how their date was going. He speculated that she was bored, that her date was much too old for her, and that she kept making 'gun-to-the-head' gestures at Jonah the whole time. At one point, I was in the middle of a sentence, and he leapt up from his stool and said, "I have to go to the bathroom! Be right back!" I turned to see that the other couple had vacated their booth.

Jonah raced in the direction of the bathrooms, presumably because he thought he was going to meet the other girl in there to compare notes. When he couldn't find her, he did a melodramatic "Which way did she go!" movement, rapidly searching the bar for her in a squat position with outstretched arms and everything. When he realized that she had exited the bar with her date instead of meeting him for a rendezvous, he returned to his seat without even attempting to make it look like he had really gone to the bathroom. He looked disappointed. I said, "I think she left," and he exclaimed, "I can't believe she would go home with a guy like that!" Like he had known this girl all his life. I began wondering if this was a joke or if this guy was actually this unbelievable.

After that, our conversation became even more enchanting. Literally ANYTHING I said he would shoot down and say he hated it. In our two hours (maybe) together I learned he hates New York City because he moved here for a girl who promptly dumped him; he hates OKCupid and has hated everyone he's met from the site; he hates sports, hates meat, hates animals, hates classic rock, hates New Mexico, hates going to bars, hates Brooklyn, and so on. Whew, this guy was exhausting! He informed me that my tattoo looks like it should be on an American Apparel T-shirt, and I noticed he had a single tiny tattoo of some sort of pill on his arm. I asked him why he was on OKCupid if he hated it so much, and he said he was looking

*for a serious girlfriend, but every girl on the site was an "aspiring
____."*

He added that he's sick of meeting girls who are bartenders or
work in retail, saying "Just be something cool now, please!" I started
to tell him that I work in retail and am happy with the direction
my life is heading at the moment, but figured it wasn't even worth
it. He went on to tell me that he might delete his OKCupid account
because it greatly offends him when ugly girls send him messages. I
asked him why and he said "Because it's insulting that they actually
think they have a chance with ME." Whoa dude. Anyone who dates
this guy would need to either be in a coma, or on eighty milligrams of
Prozac.

Surprisingly, he picked up the tab before making one last run to
the restroom. I looked at the receipt and noticed that the bartender
had given us a free round, and he still only tipped her 10 percent.
I went from strongly disliking this guy to accepting that he was
probably the worst person on the planet. I pulled aside the bartender
and said, "I'm so sorry. I'm on a blind date with this guy, he just
left you a horrible tip, and I don't have any cash." She told me not
to worry about it because I go in there all the time (it's down the
street from my work), and she knows I'm not a bad tipper. When
he returned, I thanked him for the keychain and got the hell out of
there.

When I got home, I googled Jonah and found his Twitter account.
Not ten minutes after we parted ways, he tweeted that his date (me)
was "boring, chubby, and judgy." Coming from the most "judgy" man
in all the land, his accusation was a little ironic. The only negative
thing I said during our "date" was that I hated it when guys used
"LOL." (I noticed later that he had previously sent me a couple "LOL"
texts, so I guess he was mad about that.) Chubby? Whatever, but the

other girl that he had been eyeing all night was definitely larger than I was. Boring? Come on! He just wasn't listening to my abundance of fascinating anecdotes because he was too busy interrupting me and scampering around the bathroom like an idiot. Naturally, after reading his tweet, I sent him a direct message on Twitter that read "Aww, and here I was falling deeply in love with you." He deleted his OKCupid account.

Langley Denton, 28, New York City, USA

Jobless and Bitter

I met a lovely Muslim boy with all the qualities I was searching for. He was such a gentleman! He even got me coffee! Then, two hours after the introductions, he texts me and tells me that he isn't working and hasn't been for eight months. I text back to say how wonderful the evening was but unfortunately I'm looking for stability (i.e., a man who works). Instead of a polite "OK," I got a full-on rant. "Who do you think you are—some princess?! You'd like some perfect little life. ..." On and on and on. He ended his tirade with, "No wonder you're single!" I simply replied, "Thanks. Wish you all the best."

Angela, 42, London, England

Date with Mr Ex Factor

I was set up on a blind date by a very good friend who I trusted to choose a date. He sounded like a decent guy who had all the right qualities: a good job, independent, and sounded adventurous. I turned up to meet him—we had decided to keep it quite casual. My first impression was that he was very good-looking and seemed nice, but that was where it would end. He had no substance to him and seemed only to talk about his ex-girlfriend. For example, I would ask him when the last time he'd been on holiday was, and he would say it was with his ex and go on in detail about how memorable his time with her was. In the end, it felt like a therapy session, and I came away feeling drained and exhausted! I left by saying I had a late-night project to work on. Needless to say, I never got in contact with him. Perhaps he needs to deal with his emotions before venturing out into the dating world.

Nancy, 33, London, England

Valentine's Date from Hell

I had been dating this professional guy who lived out of London and was invited out for Valentine's. We had a lovely three-course meal dinner date. I began to feel a little tired. He invited me back to his place in Luton, which I declined due to the fact that I believed I was not ready to go to that stage! He then suggested we go to his mother's or a bar/club to continue getting to know one another. As I was tired, I insisted on being taken home. I was very full by this time!

Instead, he drove me to his mother's house and attempted to force me out of the car and onto the road as I refused to go inside. I then attempted to call a taxi as I was left stranded on a random road in a red dress being harassed by males. I now always make sure I drive to any dates!

Lee-Sha, 29, London, England

Red Flags

The first quote that came to mind after reading these stories was one of my favourite quotes from Maya Angelou, "*When people show you who they really are, believe them.*" All the men highlighted in the dates above displayed and waved that red flag high above their heads on date 1. These sensible ladies didn't think, "Oh, let's give him one more chance" or "Perhaps it was an off day." They took the message delivered to them loud and clear and moved on. If this is how they treat women on date 1, what hope is there for any type of long-term (or even short-term) commitment?

Ms Won't Date a Co-Worker Again offered to pay her half of the bill at the start, yet her date insisted on paying. Dates should not come with conditions. If a man invites you out on a date and offers to pay, then that is exactly what should occur regardless. Women are not possessions to be bought. She showed grace and integrity when paying her share of the bill. Asking a date for money after not receiving a little 'something' in return? Code Red Flag!

Milton the Mortician and Judgemental Jonah, (both Mr Loose Eyes) shared a severe lack of grace or decency when actively checking out other girls both on OkCupid Apps and in the bar. A sure red flag! Credit to Langley who dealt with these men with both humour and wit.

Similarly, Mr Jobless and Bitter quickly showed his date his true colours via the use of his text attack. Every woman and man alive has a right to their individual needs, expectations, and standards. Needing and wanting your man to have a job and some stability in his life is not a crime. Far from it. This should tell this man everything he needs to know. This lady places stability and security high on her agenda of needs and wants and actively seeks to see the bigger picture: a future. Instead of respecting this woman's standards, he attacked her and accused her of being a princess.

Lee-Sha again dealt with this situation with integrity and humility by not engaging in his accusations and unprovoked tirade but by wishing him the best and closing the door. Red Flag seen, acknowledged, and dealt with!

One thing we need to remember when going on dates is: keep it light, keep it free, keep it simple. Your date does not need to know about your ex-boyfriends, previous drink addiction, or psychological effects of an unhealthy relationship on date one. Save that for when they have earned your confidence and earned your trust. If you have a deep yearning to talk about this, talk to a trusted friend, family member, or counsellor. Your date is not there to give you a therapy session. Your date is there to get to know you slowly. Dating should be fun, exciting, and light. If you are battling with demons or not over a relationship, perhaps you are not yet ready to date. Some people think that after a break-up or trauma, the best thing to do is to "get back out there into the dating world." However, they make the fatal mistake of unleashing all their hurt, angst, and dilemmas upon the poor, unsuspecting date. Don't be a Ms Ex Factor. I am a staunch believer that in order to give someone the best of ourselves, we must heal past hurts and issues residing within. If you end up being counsellor or therapist on your first date, don't expect to have an equal relationship. I would charge them a fee and run!!

Mr Valentine's Date From Hell's behaviour is truly despicable. Just because he paid for a three-course meal does not give him licence to expect the relationship to suddenly turn physical. He needs to learn, as does our Mister from Dinner Date, that women are not commodities. If a man invites a woman out to a restaurant—or anywhere—then he has, without conditions, committed to paying the bill without expectations. If you have arranged an alternative plan with your date (i.e., 50/50 payment, or that a starter is equal to a peck on the cheek, a main course a snog, and ... you get my drift), then that is another story!

Nonetheless forcing a woman out of a car in an unknown area, in the dead of night is unacceptable. This inexcusable behaviour is only testament to his character. This man flew a red flag as red as this poor woman's dress, yet it's given her a degree of independence. Always drive to dates with men you do not fully know or trust, or take public transport. I wonder how his mother would have felt about his behaviour, although something tells me that she wasn't even in!

Mr. Prescreening

I was thrilled during my first date with this gentleman, a guy I'd connected with on a dating site. We had many common interests and an absolutely scintillating conversation over dinner. He kissed me good night when he dropped me off at my home and told me he'd had a magnificent time. Needless to say, I was surprised not to hear from him again. Two months later, he rang me and said he'd like to see me again. I told him honestly that I was very shocked to hear from him. He asked why. "Well," I explained, "When you didn't ask me for a second date, I figured you weren't interested in me and had moved on."

"What do you mean 'second date'?" he asked.

"The night we met was our first date," I responded.

"What? That wasn't a date," he argued.

"Then what was it?" I asked.

He said, "That was just a meeting."

"Oh. Well, in that case, I guess if we go out now, that'll be our first date, right?" I asked jovially.

"No, no!" he corrected. "It's not going to be a date, it's going to be a pre-dating screening," adding—as if it were obvious—"I still don't know you nearly well enough yet to know if I'd like to date you!"

"OK," I said, clarifying, "so we've had a meeting, and then I'm on to the pre-dating screening, and if all that goes well, then you might ask me for a date?"

"Yes," he said, "but I'm certainly not rushing into anything. This process could take a couple months or more. Don't you understand? I have to get to know you."

"But isn't that what dating IS?" I countered.

Was I dating him or applying for a mortgage? Since I wasn't sure, I declined his offer.

Marie, 46, Hull, Massachusetts, USA

Screening Your Date vs Getting to Know Your Date

Dating should be fun and light and easy. It gives both parties an opportunity to get to know each other. Mr Pre-screener took this to another level! Whilst being cautious and taking your time is important when finding the right partner, it is equally important to ensure the person does not feel like they are in an interview or taking part in an assessment of some sort. Dating should take place in a relaxed environment where both parties can be themselves and feel at ease. Compatibility will either be there or it won't, and the last thing you need is to feel as if you have been sat on stage to be judged and screened for the X Factor or that you are attending a casting for the next Hollywood movie! If Marie had been lucky enough to go through to the final round, she may even have had 'girlfriend' status in a couple of years!

Quiz Time!

What type of date are you looking for?

_____

_____

_____

_____

_____

What are the qualities you look for in a man?

_____

_____

_____

_____

_____

What are the "red flags" for you?

_____

_____

_____

_____

_____

Have you ever spotted any of these red flags on the first few dates and carried on?

_____

_____

_____

_____

_____

How did the experience progress?

_____

_____

_____

_____

Would you react differently now? How?

_____

_____

_____

_____

Question Time!

What would you like to find out about your date before going on date number two? Write a list of 10 questions you would like to ask your date. Think about your values and what is important to you. NB. This does not mean you have to reel them off one after the other, interview style. Be discreet. Remember, these questions can always be answered during natural dialogue with your date. My top two questions would be as follows:

Is family important to you?

How do you usually spend your free time?

1)

2)

3)

4)

5)

6)

7)

8)

9)

10)

Now look back at these questions and write down the answers. Is this man compatible with you? Do his actions support his answers as time progresses?

Good Luck! :)

Chapter 4: Mr Dreamer on Social Media

To fish or not to fish? That is the question. Like it or not, Internet dating is now one of the fastest-growing phenomena in the world. Can true love be found online? Or are these dating sites full of Mr Wrongs masquerading under a pumped-up profile? According to The Huffington Post,[1] online dating is a £2bn industry. With over half the UK's singletons participating in Internet dating, Huffington Post states, "Online dating is now so important to the UK economy that the Office of National Statistics recently added online dating to its basket of goods and services to calculate UK inflation rates." Globally, one in five relationships start via online dating, and there are constantly stories in the media detailing happy marriages sparked by online dating subscriptions. With over 7'500 sites available globally, online dating can be a great way to connect people to each other from all over the world, matching people with similar likes, dislikes, interests, and relationship needs and wants.

However this is not always the case. Whilst online dating sites can be largely positive and have greatly enhanced communication globally, the rise of social media in general has also diminished the art of personal, face-to-face communication.

---

[1] Taken from Charlie Thomas' article The £2bn Relationship - The Business Of Online Dating posted 27th October 2012

The anonymity that social sites provide allows the user to be just that—a user. The anonymity not only allows some users to create a brand-new personality for themselves, but at times a complete life transplantation! How many times have you gone on a date with a "mature, kind-hearted, toned Don Juan" who works as a Fitness Instructor only to find out he is a tight fisted, sweaty man-child who works at your local fishmongers? Now there is nothing wrong with working at a fishmongers but it's not exactly what you ordered was it? It is disheartening to find that your "Don Juan's" six-pack is really a six pack of beer each night. The internet is easy to hide behind. And sadly, when this life transplantation is discovered by the unwitting victim, a simple click of the "delete" button from the game-playing catfish can erase all responsibility as the victim sinks back into the pool of fungus and fish.

Having been a user of dating websites such as Match.com and Plenty of Fish.com, it seems to me there are too many perfectly good women in their late twenties and thirties swimming solo in the lonely ocean where there simply are not plenty of fish. There are, however, plenty of sharks lurking at the bottom, ready to devour and spit them out with a virtual "poke," "block," or simple "deletion" from their lives via social media. What happened to chivalry, sticking power, respect, and honesty? What happened to looking someone in the eyes and telling them what they really mean, really feel?

Whilst I embrace technology, I do feel that with the influx of dating sites, obtaining a date/girlfriend/

one-nighter/casual relationship/hookup is becoming as simple as reciting the ABC. In some cases, it's become even easier than buying a pair of shoes online! Now, as a single lady I see nothing wrong with this as we are all busy people and why not shop for a man online? We shop online for clothes, books, DVDs, and home and kitchen ware. Why not shop for a man who has credentials for all to see—likes, wants, compatibility test, chemistry test, you name it!? It can be much easier than meeting a man in a bar, club, or by chance. However, at times it gets to the point where you just want to give the "potential" a questionnaire to fill in about himself before you even chat. It can get tiresome getting to know someone only to find out a few weeks or months later he is a raging homophobic, hates children, and worse still, doesn't like Caribbean cuisine.

Sadly, it feels we have lost the art of communication. It just seems to me that we are now living in a nation where we are too quick to put our profile online and too scared to put our hearts on the line. Breaking up via text, BBM, Facebook and other sources of social media is becoming the norm, and good old, honest face-to-face conversations are running out of trend. Why do we have to find out we've been dumped via a "Block" or a "Blog"? Even sometimes via "air"! Simple silence. What does this say about the growth of human interaction? Real interaction. Real communication. 'I love you' is now replaced with 'I heart you' or via a cyber-rose or flying cupid heart. Words, emotions, hearts lost in translation. Hearts bruised via diminished responsibility.

The heart of what I am saying here is that I believe we are becoming a nation full of quick fixes where responsibility for our decisions and actions can be obscured and replaced by a quick press of a keyboard or click of a button. More and more people, both men and women, are being dumped by text, mobile, or some other source of social media, taking away personal contact and empathy. As I say, I embrace technology; however, on the flip side, this reliance on technology stops us from facing up to things, leaving us devoid of emotion and compassion. Technology cannot replace sincerity.

The stories below all highlight relationships that have begun online and ended via the power of technology.

My trigger for writing this book was an experience I had with a man known in the cyber world as JudgeJustice. I had broken up with the man I believed to be my soul mate, and I was walking around a right old mess. I signed up to a dating site and met a guy called JudgeJustice. He was a Mr Dreamer—full on in the beginning and a "vanisher" after the three-month marker. I had no idea what I had done wrong or to deserve this treatment, but when it happened, I just knew I had to write this book.

What was different about this break-up was, although I liked this man very much, I hadn't allowed myself to fully fall. When the "disappearance" happened, I knew so strongly that it was not my fault. I knew that I was not the cause of the break–up, that there was nothing wrong with me, and that I was worthy of being loved. What JudgeJustice did do was distract me from the pain of my break-up and so allowed me to heal through laughter and showing me love. In hindsight, I was perhaps subconsciously unavailable myself.

Although we'd had a great time, he disappeared like a magician's handkerchief and after questioning what was going on I was dumped via a short text with no explanation. Shortly after his disappearance and text, he gave me a sincere apology on the phone. This made it easy for me to forgive him and move on without negative feelings or bitterness. It was at this point that so many of my friends began to tell me I should write a book. It was at this point I realised that people really do come into our lives for a reason, a season, a lesson, and a blessing. I would never in my wildest dreams have imagined I'd put myself out there like this, but I feel if my stories and experiences can help others realise that it is our attitude towards break-ups, relationships and attitudes towards ourselves that should change and not us, then I feel it has all been worth it. A year after the event, JudgeJustice called me up and apologised again. He explained that he had an issue with commitment. He was surprised that I held absolutely no resentment. It is this releasing of resentment that is key to everything. It does not mean we have to accept them back, it means that we are free from blame and bitterness. JudgeJustice taught me to forgive quickly and not punish myself with blame and feelings of unworthiness. I hope this book helps you to do the same.

Judge Justice

After a string of bad luck with guys and a very recent heartbreak, I decided (more like I was persuaded) to set up a profile and join the merry world of Internet dating—after all, there's plenty of fish in the sea! I met a guy who called himself Judge Justice. Ironic—but we'll come to that! We chatted for a bit and seemed to hit it off really well. He was one of the first who didn't send me simple one-liners such as "How are you, babes?" or use terrible teenage text speak such as "wot u up 2. U on bbm? Lol." No, he could actually string a sentence together and I was happy. We went on a few dates, and I wasn't sure about him at first, partly because I was still healing from a painful break-up and partly because that "je ne sais quoi" was missing. However, he appeared very keen on me, and he seemed funny, kind, and generous and full of compliments.

As most of them do at the beginning, he put on a great act of being the perfect gentleman—opening car doors, restaurant doors, and slowly opening the door to my heart. We would speak for hours, and he would tell me what a diamond I was. In fact, I quote, "a diamond that shouldn't be locked in a cupboard but looked after and treasured." He told me how lucky he felt to be next to me and how beautiful I was. He even asked me if I thought he was "the one." He'd hold my hand and take me to comedy clubs and restaurants. He said that I deserved to be treated well, and I finally began letting him in. Although at first I wasn't sure, it all changed when he came round to my house by date four or five with some kitchen lights he'd noticed needed changing. Now these weren't just any bulbs- these were expensive and hard to find. From here, I was hooked in and I began to think, well, perhaps he is the one.

When we'd first got together, he was working and studying to gain a qualification that would grant him a lot more responsibility in his current position. After four weeks of being together, he'd passed, and being a 21st-century woman, I took him out for dinner to celebrate and say well done. Then, coming up to the two-month marker, he'd seemed to ease into comfortability. Suddenly, he didn't need to call me every night and spend hours on the phone. Suddenly, he was working away much more and putting more hours in. I am a supportive woman and so encouraged him with his new job. However, instead of hours between our conversations, it was days. Sometimes there wasn't even a text to say good night or reply back to my texts. Seven weeks in, we'd spent every weekend together—all at his initiation. It all started to go wrong after we'd gone two weeks without seeing each other. Phone calls were now a rarity due to both of our busy schedules and demanding jobs. It so happened that work got more stressful for both of us.

One Saturday he came round, and I promised I'd cook him a nice home-cooked meal as I knew he'd not had one living in hotels for the last four weeks (weekdays). I was looking forward to seeing him; however, instead of being greeted with the usual happy smile and cuddle, I felt a distinct coldness or perhaps nonchalance. As I cut the vegetables, he asked causally if I'd watch football with him. I swallowed my annoyance and sweetly said, "Yeah, of course. I'll try fifteen/twenty minutes and see how I go." (In case you hadn't gleaned from this, I can't stand watching the game. To me, it's like watching paint dry.) I tried and that was the main thing. Little did I know that he meant right there and then. So before I knew it, within ten minutes of him being at my house, he'd switched off my ambient music, crawled into my room, and switched on the football—and there I was, cutting his carrots in the kitchen whilst being subjected to incessant foghorns and chanting. Not the romantic evening I had planned! In a more long-term relationship, that would be fine (semi-

fine), but two months in and not having seen each other for two weeks—you're havin' a laugh!

So how did this football fanatic become Mr Wrong? Well, after he left the following morning, I didn't hear a peep from him. Not a sausage. He slept round on the Saturday and was silent from Sunday through to Friday. I called him on Thursday and got no reply. I left a text to see if he was OK. No answer. I called again on the following Friday only to hear the ring tone from abroad. I could not believe it. I could not believe he would bugger off abroad and not tell me or even say good-bye. By this time my inclination was right. This man was no longer interested. He'd eaten his cake and was now sniffing around for another.

I sent a text letting him know I was ringing to ask how he was and that it seems he is abroad. I explained that from his lack of communication I understood that he no longer wanted to continue dating and that I felt he respected and cared about me enough to let me know instead of leaving me hanging. I explained that I expected more and that I had enjoyed our time together and ended by wishing him an enjoyable time abroad and wishing him the best to which he simply replied, "Thanks babe so sorry. Xx good luck you deserve better than me. Please forgive me and move on Xx," to which I replied, "Damn right I deserve better. Either before you get back or personally when you get back, I would like an explanation. I am worth more than a text, so I hope and appreciate you doing the right thing and calling me and communicating with me properly."

This was the first time I'd ever opened my heart to rejection and simply asked for what I wanted—an explanation. It was also the first time I actually believed I deserved better. Really believed. I did get my phone call a week later, complete with mutterings about work being full on and it not being fair to keep me in a relationship he couldn't commit to etc., etc. He admitted to being a coward. I thanked him for the three-minute phone call and wished him luck on his path. That is the last time I cook my Caribbean curried chicken for just anybody!

Now why is the name JudgeJustice ironic? Because I was not the best judge of character, and at the time I felt a great sense of injustice!

Thank you JudgeJustice for teaching me how to forgive and teaching me the importance of clarity.

Daniella, 34, London, England

Mr Wrong Has Parents' Evening – The Ex Factor

My experience with Jez came after a string of let downs and Mr Wrongs. I met Jez on Match.com and we hit it off immediately. He was a teacher, and I was attracted to his knowledge and passion for his job. The first date we went to a pub, the second date to the cinema, and the third date he came to my house and cooked me dinner. Cooking me dinner, I thought, felt like the beginnings of a relationship. He would do sweet things like kiss me on my forehead and say things you would only really say in relationships. By the fourth date, we slept together. I should have seen the Ex Factor lurking in the background pretty soon after he said, "It's so strange sleeping with someone new."

After our fifth date I began to feel that the relationship was one-sided. I'd never been to his house or been introduced to any part of his life in any way. I also realised that the space in between dates became bigger and bigger; his schedule became busier, and he began cancelling dates last minute, saying that "important commitments" had arisen. We went from a couple of dates a week to a date every week and a half. I felt almost as if I wasn't a priority. Promises he'd made at the beginning, such as things we'd do in the future, became an illusion; false promises were being made and broken. I spotted the signs, and then I received a text one morning cancelling dinner at mine that evening. He wasn't to know that I was left with a fridge full of fancy food that didn't fit into my normal repertoire of pasta and rice. He didn't know I'd gone and bought things like sweet basil, mascarpone, and vanilla pods, but who cancels last minute like that?! His text simply said, "Sorry, I will have to cancel tonight due to a parents' evening I'd forgotten. How about a nice meal at the weekend instead?"

Although his text seemed pretty genuine, I'd already been accustomed to the tell-tale signs of Mr Unavailable, so I rang him up and said, "What's going on?" to which he replied, "No, it's fine. I've honesty got parents' evening."

Giving him an outlet, I said, "Look, I'm getting the impression that you're not interested. Is that the case?" For some reason he seemed to think it was easier to spin me around for another two weeks as he protested, "No, no, no. I like you. I'm just busy and we should still see each other at the weekend."

What Mr Wrong didn't realise was that I was a busy girl too and that I didn't want to make weekend plans only for them to be cancelled again. Furthermore, I'm not stupid. I know when someone's not interested. Most women do. It's called women's intuition. So I gave him another get-out-of-jail-free card and asked him again if he was sure he wanted to meet, to which he replied, "Of course." Undeterred, I asked if he had a recent ex on the scene, to which he relented and said, "Yes, you're right. I've just come out of a long-term relationship. I get the impression that you want a relationship, and I'm not really in that space at the moment." As he said this, I thought to myself, I was the one who wanted to take things slowly, and he was the one who was acting as if we were in a relationship. How did the shoe switch onto the other foot?!

Instead, I just told him that I understood. He felt the need to reassure me by telling me that he thought I was a great girl and that he wanted to take things slowly and would still love to meet on Sunday.

Later that day, he sent a text saying, "I think your a great girl but don think we shld see each other on Sunday," to which I replied, "Thank you very much. Just wanted you to know I was just following your lead. I wish you good luck on your journey." And that was the last I heard of Jez. It hurt so much, not only because he had chosen to communicate with me via text—albeit it with bad grammar too!—but because he led me to believe that he wanted a relationship. When I finally let him in and opened myself up and became vulnerable to him, he let me down with a bump. And for the record, I later discovered that there was no parents' evening at all.

I think I would have been more distraught if it wasn't for his hideous grammar!

Andrea, 30, Milton Keynes, England

Cursed Out

I don't think I had met anyone from Yonkers before I met Tommy. He looked happy and well-balanced in his photos, with a shaved head and an earring. Tommy was a big sports fan and seemed to possess some of the traditional notions that many of my Italian-American friends did. I liked the fact that he was easy to talk to on *the phone, sounded like a complete gentleman with a street-smart manner.*

After a couple of phone conversations, we decided to meet for a drink. At the time, both of us were in school and I was working full-time as well, so while it is always nerve-wracking to meet someone face-to-face for the first time, it would be a fun way to break up the week.

I got to the bar first and when Tommy walked in, a few minutes later, I knew it was him but my heart pretty much sank. Yes, there was a resemblance to his photos but you just never get the full idea of someone's presence until you meet in person. His teeth were not the greatest and the 'Cosby sweater' he was wearing didn't help matters.

Tommy and I got along fairly well. The conversation flowed naturally, mostly because the vodka tonics kept flowing as well. I certainly was not attracted to him and since I've never possessed the power of flirtation, I don't think I led him to believe that I was at all. We touched on a topic at one point that is a commonly-understood "no-no" for first dates and that was exes. Tommy said some fairly rude things about his most recent girlfriend, which led me to believe (among a few other comments) that he was of the angry persuasion. I smiled and politely continued listening and communicating. We even had a moment outside the bar where we smooched a bit. Hey, I'm only human. Things happen. But it was certainly no big deal and we eventually walked to the closest train station and said our goodbyes My feeling is that you can never know for sure how the other person felt about it and if you will ever communicate with them again.

Tommy ended up sending me a text message the evening after we met. I had just walked into a class and was settling in when he wrote, 'When can I see you again?'

Crap,' I thought. I knew we weren't going to see one another again, and wanted to be truthful, but polite. I don't deal very well when my feelings are ignored, so I opt to be straightforward the majority of the time in situations like these.

As my professor began the evening's lecture, I messaged Tommy back, typing, 'Hey there. It was great meeting you. I just don't think we are a good match. Take care!' Incidentally, the last guy I had gone on a date with before Tommy had written something like that to me. I was interested in him, but he didn't feel the same. His answer stung a little, but I appreciated the fact that he answered me honestly.

Tommy didn't share that opinion. 'Wow, are you f**king kidding me?!? You're one crazy-ass bitch!'

Shaken a bit (and sitting in a tiny, silent classroom), I responded nicely by saying, 'I just don't think it would work out. Thanks for understanding.'

Tommy: 'You kiss all your dates? No wonder you're single – you're f**king nuts!'

Me: 'You take care now.'

Tommy: 'F**k you, you crazy bitch.'

Me: 'Thanks!'

Thankfully, I didn't hear from Tommy again, but that experience definitely unnerved me. I really hope that Tommy's future dates were attracted to him. Otherwise, these women were definitely in for a treat.

Gena Robyn, 35, New York, USA

The Importance of Being Earnest

The first two stories highlight men who have presented all the factors and displayed all the actions of someone who wanted a full-blown relationship yet in the end became confused and changed their minds. Everyone has the right to change their mind or want something different; it's human nature. But the scar of being lied to or being made to feel inadequate or not deserving of that truth is what hurts the most. The damage of not having been empowered with that little bit of clarity or honesty or even the respect of mutual communication is what disempowers the woman; it makes them feel inadequate and not deserving enough of the truth. That lack of clarity or earnestness is what deprives a person of their ability to feel part of that choice or discussion. Sometimes the downfall of meeting people online is that it is easy to sink back into anonymity and obscurity.

In the case of JudgeJustice, if he hadn't been so full on with the hearts and flowers to start with, if he had taken it slowly, they both could have connected at a pace they were both comfortable with without rushing anything. There is nothing wrong with being full on, but if he is a Mr Dreamer, providing nothing but false hope and fanciful words without the ability to treat a woman with the respect, honesty, and decency she deserves, then my advice would be to leave him in the land of nod. In essence, Mr Dreamer perhaps has good intentions; however, he is just unable to see them through. The key is for him to be honest about his positive intentions and wishes for the future but also to have the integrity to be clear and honest about them when they change. Certainly in my case with JudgeJustice, I remember feeling as though I had been betrayed somehow and I felt like a prize fool. I had finally let someone in and they let me down, not with the truth but with the lack of it. It seems it isn't the decision that hurts so much in this instance; it's the lack of clarity and communication. To women, the importance of being earnest is everything.

In the case of Jez, if he had been honest about what he wanted and needed from the start—and more so when Andrea gave him the opportunity to be honest—it would have saved a great deal of pain. Instead of going to great lengths to lie and cover up how he really felt and what he really wanted, thinking he was saving a woman from feeling hurt, he should have just been honest. By stringing along a woman he was unable to satisfy, he was depriving her of finding real happiness. Women don't want men to sugar-coat things. We just want honesty.

In *Cursed Out* Gena tried to respectfully let Tommy know that it wouldn't work between them. This act was out of respect for his feelings and a desire to be honest with him. Instead of taking it on the chin and accepting Gena's wishes, Tommy became abusive via text. It is ok to change our minds and decide that this person is not for us, particularly after one date! Gena admits to knowing how hurtful it is to have your feelings ignored and so thought that honesty was best in this case. We have the right to express how we feel and what we want or don't want. Tommy's gross overreaction proved that he is most certainly not the right person for her (or anybody right now for that matter). Judging by the topic of conversation, it seems that he either doesn't have very much respect for women or is carrying some heavy baggage from his relationship with his ex. Code red flag!

Sudden disappearances are typical behaviour traits of Mr Dreamer and Mr Ex Factors. These men offer the shortest ride at the funfair. A fast-paced build-up followed by an abrupt ending via text, email, or other forms of social media are sadly what these Mr Wrongs tend to offer. Sadly, that lack of clarity, honesty, and face-to-face communication at worst can compromise and deprive a woman of her integrity and often her sense of self-worth. What we must realise is that we mustn't blame ourselves for others' actions or cowardice or failure to even face their truth themselves; we must know that we are worth more and deserve better and—at best—ensure we don't stoop to their level. Gena, knowing what it was like to have her feelings ignored, respectfully sent her date an honest text however although she was not thanked for this she did the right thing and most importantly, even when he was cursing and insulting, kept her sense if integrity. Do not be defined by their treatment of you. Wish them good luck on their journey and move on. Always keep your sense of integrity intact. Below is a story demonstrating the importance of being frank and earnest. And guess what? The man survived!

"I'm Just Not that into You" Texts

We are not always going to meet the soul mate of our dreams right away, and yes, this means being honest with them and letting them know you are not interested in the most tactful and sensitive way you can. We don't want to cause offence, but equally we don't want to lead anyone on or, worse still, leave them hanging. Below, Sally has a perfect example of a polite, "I'm just not that into you text."

Thanks, But No Thanks: A is for Adam

"So, yeah, that's it, really. That's me in a nutshell." He looks nervous, this man I'm having coffee with. He's fidgeting and having trouble keeping eye contact. I don't know if it's something about me, or if it's something about him. I'm on a date, the first one in nearly three years, and I'm out of practice. I've forgotten how prepared I need to be, how ready I need to be to pick up the conversation. He's a friend of Kira's, and she's set us up. "You guys might just work together," she said to me.

He's good-looking, this man, with a great smile, a rugged build, and impressive biceps. (He displays said muscles when he pulls up his sleeve to show me the tattoos on his arms: a Canadian flag, a set of stylized Hawaiian turtles, a '66 Mustang—just like the one in his garage.) His arms are beautiful: he might be worth a second date just for his body. He's funny too, and wealthy and adventurous. Really, what's not to like?

But he's not for me.

And the most surprising thing about this realization is that I'm not disappointed. I'm relieved. It is so good to know that I haven't lost my judgement, to know that I can trust my instincts, to know that I'm not going to end up in a relationship unless it's just right.

I'm also out of practice about saying no. But it's something I'm going to have to get good at. I'm sure that I'm going to have to say no many times before I get to say yes. So, starting now, I'm going to document my "Thanks, but no thanks" texts.

A is for Adam

Hi Adam,

Thank you so much for coffee today. I enjoyed your sense of humour and appreciated your honesty. And—I have to say—those are impressive biceps. Honestly, I'm surprised you're still single. But I don't think it's going to work out for us. I'm an island girl, and I need someone who wants to be here, who isn't trying to escape this place.

I wish you well, Adam.

Sally, Canada

"Just Not that into You" Texts Exercise

Just as we know how awful it can be to date somebody and suddenly never hear from them again, we too have a responsibility to provide our date with honesty and respect. Sally's message is perfect; complimentary but candid about her needs I, too, have my own standard default "Just Not into You" text.

"It was great to meet you. I think you are (fill in appropriate compliment if you have one!), and I really enjoyed (fill in accurate activity). However, unfortunately I don't think we clicked romantically. I wish you well finding your Ms Right.

I like this as it is non-emotional and not personal. You are simply thanking him for his time and appreciating his company but being honest about your intentions at the same time. You can only really receive a positive response to this unless your date decides to hit you with a barrage of texts telling you how wrong you are about your decision and that you DID click romantically, in which case block his number ASAP!

Use the space below to construct your own "Just Not that into You" Text.

_____

_____

_____

_____

_____

_____

_____

_____

_____

Chapter 5: Mr Serial Liar

The Serial Liars are often one of the hardest men to shake off. The reason? They make you doubt yourself, question your own sense of what is true, as well as your powerful intuition. These men have lying down to an art form, and as a result, at worst, they have you questioning your own sanity. These men are extremely manipulative and incapable of offering you what you truly need, want, and deserve. These men offer you relationships like The Waltzer and Rollercoaster. Whilst you are so taken by the ride, he continues to lie, cheat, and deceive; however, when you start to smell the rat on the ride, he will either cover his tracks by lying, making it seem like your fault, or by simply disappearing.

You cannot and will not change someone who is this manipulative and dishonest. This is learnt behaviour, and change can only come through their desire to change themselves. If we are putting up with men who constantly lie and deceive us, the question must then be asked, what motivation do they have to change? If we are putting up with men who repeatedly lie, cheat, and deceive us, what message are we sending them about our own values and sense of self-worth?

I have experienced Mr Serial Liar only once and once was enough. Unfortunately I didn't sniff out his lie until nearly a year after we broke up. In the end I felt nothing but pity that this man must have been so unhappy he felt the need to lead a double life and lie and deceive those whom he was supposed to love. Most of all, I felt a great sense of relief that my intuition was right. From there on in, I learnt to listen to the dreams, messages, and small voice within that since a very small child has guided me through the darkness and away from dishonesty and negativity. For it wasn't the small voice within that was wrong, but my lack of desire to interpret and understand my intuition and uncover the horrible truth. I have decided to share my story on the next page.

Mr Duplicitous

I met a guy at a club in London. Let's call him LP (Lying Professional). He was a doorman. Already I hear the words chime in ... How cliché! Of course he's a ladies' man. Well, I hadn't been with anyone for a very long time, and we got talking and really hit it off. I never give my number out, but on this occasion I decided to. The following day I received a text from him, and we quickly struck up conversation on the phone. We arranged a date. Although we did not have firm plans, it was still a date. We planned to meet up in Central London around 7 p.m., and we left it that we would talk and arrange a place. Now, as the day came up, I had decided what I was going to wear, etc. However, when I hadn't heard from him by 5 p.m., I smelt a rat. Now, I'm a woman who doesn't like her time being wasted, so I called him to find out what was going on only to repeatedly get voicemail.

I cracked a bottle of wine out with the girls instead; however, one of my pet hates is people who go back on their word, leave you hanging, and let you down last minute, let alone not even bother to contact you. Simple manners! As I said, I am a woman who does not like her time being wasted. When he finally called the following day apologising, he explained that he was picking his mum up at the airport (delayed flight, of course) and had no reception and then his battery must have died. But it was too late. I had already made up my mind that he was undateable and made that very clear.

A few weeks later, I lost a close relative unexpectedly and was having trouble coming to terms with this as anyone would. In the midst of all this, he called apologising, and I explained that I wasn't able to talk as I'd lost someone dear to me and was not able to deal with the conversation. From herein, he was fantastic. He became a real friend to me, ringing me, talking to me, sending me comforting texts and jokes at night as I couldn't sleep. He even turned up at my university with a big bunch of flowers. Feeling vulnerable, I appreciated his gestures and support and we began to date. It was great. We would go on romantic boat rides, visit London Dungeons, The Aquarium, frequent expensive restaurants, and go to the cinema. He would not let me pay for anything. This was so far removed from what I was used to, and for the first time in my life I felt like a queen. We would talk three, four times a day at length and see each other every weekend without fail. As we both had very busy schedules, I was happy with this and quite liked the not-having-to-see-each-other-every-day intensity.

However, in the fifth month he moved out from the flat he said he shared with his brother and moved in with his mum (!) at the grand old age of 33. During this time he became "ill", working two jobs and generally running here, there, and everywhere. Plans were arranged and cancelled last minute, plans became hazy, and he became flaky. I'd offered to come and look after him but ... oh no, he did not want to burden me with that! Eventually it all came to a head when we had arranged to meet up one day and again he cancelled last minute. This started our first and only argument. My fatal mistake was to dare to say that I was upset that he could not be consistent. My punishment? A refusal to answer my calls or texts and completely ignore my existence for a total of three days! I think this did more damage than anything. Being ignored is far worse than somebody being honest with you or even shouting a few words of anger. To be ignored is the ultimate hurt for me. It's very personal.

After three days I texted him and simply asked if he was OK as I was worried. I asked him just to reply to let me know he was OK. I received a text saying, "I'm ok." Having fallen for this man, I texted him the following day, apologising, to show that I understood that he was going through "stress at work" and that's why he couldn't commit to plans. I told him that no matter what, I'd loved spending time with him and that I would always cherish the memories we'd had together (as if his ego needed any more stroking!). To this, he replied eagerly, "Oh the power of words. ..." something ... something irrelevant, like he was no longer angry at me and that he was willing to give it another go! Lucky me! Although I say this now, I was happy at the time.

We continued to date, and the same flaky behaviour kept happening. After not having seen each other for a good three weeks or more, we had arranged that he would look at his "work schedule" and see if we could meet up that evening or perhaps the next. Well, most people would think that meant that they would receive a phone call during the day to confirm a possible arrangement during the evening. However, not LP. He called me past 9 p.m. saying that he had been at the gym, hence not having called. When I dared to ask why he had not called me during the day to say that this evening would be a write-off as he was going to the gym instead, he screamed at me down the phone. He accused me of nagging him and not understanding the stress he was going through before shouting at me to forget the whole thing and hanging up at me. I am a woman of peace, and although devastated, I sent a text telling him it was a shame to have ended this way, and I thanked him for the time we spent together. I never heard from LP again. Well … not until a year or so later.

A year or so later I made a shocking discovery. I discovered the root of his "stress," "illness," and "anxiety." I discovered that during our whole eight-month 'relationship'—for I use that term loosely— he was in fact engaged to his long-term partner with a child. This I found out via a social networking site. We ended our relationship in March, and he was due to marry in August. I felt sick to my stomach and, most of all, hated myself for being such a terrible judge of character. He actually had the audacity to contact me a few years later telling me how upset he was that we ended and that everything seemed to end when we broke up. I asked him if he was married yet or engaged, and he told me the only thing he was attached to was his job. I eventually sent him an email attaching pictures I'd found of his wedding day. Funnily enough, I haven't heard from the rat since!

On another note—your subconscious is a very powerful thing. Within the first two months of dating LP, I had a dream that there were two of him. One was carrying a safe and had a chain/lock around his ankle; at the time I did not give it a second thought. (I think I even told him!) It wasn't until years later I realised that the safe was his "secret" and the lock symbolised that he was already settled or 'committed' to someone else. The reason there were two of him? Well, he was a duplicitous rat!

This experience sadly strengthened a sense of unworthiness within myself. I was treated like I was the most special person in the world at a time I felt vulnerable and was dropped unceremoniously with no explanation. Finding out he was a Serial Liar gave me a strange sense of relief. It was then I recognised that we should never define ourselves or judge our worth by someone else's treatment of us. I felt sorry for this man. This was an awakening for me. In my mind I forgave him and most importantly I forgave myself for blaming and beating myself up believing myself to be unworthy. I learned to listen to my inner voice and discern. I learned to start to recognise my own worth. Thank you LP for starting me on that journey.

Daniella, 34, London, England

Mr D and His Web of Lies

I was on my way home one evening with friends when a car pulled up aside with eyes fixated in my direction. We were neck to neck at the traffic lights. The window winds down and the driver asks for directions. I politely respond and go on my way. I pulled up in a petrol station and noticed the driver followed suit. He walked over and we began speaking. This is the night I would meet Mr D. After exchanging numbers, several dates, and being seduced by his charms, I actually started to like Mr D. He wasn't my usual type, but then again, my usual type hadn't been working for me either. What was there to lose? I was young, single, enjoyed my job; life was good. The only negative was that he lived quite a distance from me (the other side of London). I drove; he drove. I decided to make it work.

Every weekend I would drive up and spend the entire week. Spending time with him was great. He was attentive, kind, and great in bed. It was fair to say I was quite content. We would spend time with his family—Sunday lunch BBQs and dinner. I felt it was moving a little fast, but great—I was going to go with the flow. I grew to really like him. He made me feel special and we got on well. There was one thing that used to puzzle me at times, and this was a vacant look in his eyes. I would ask, but he would say it was the pressure of opening his new business. Living so far apart and not knowing anything about him other than what he and his family had told me, I had to trust him. I had no other reason not to.

After seeing each other for about five months, his communication with me became sloppy (below what I would consider acceptable). Date nights were cancelled, my visits became less frequent. I am by no means a bunny boiler, but something had shifted. He reassured me that it was the pressure of starting his new business as there had been unexpected delays. I understood to a certain degree, but it came to a point where I had to cool it off. He became more and more unreliable, and the arguments became more frequent. This was no longer fun, and his failed promises became too much.

I didn't hear from him for a while, and during this time I bought a new phone and new number. After about four months after we went our separate ways, my friend calls me and tells me that Mr D had called her asking for my number. I said, 'OK, you can give it to him.' I wasn't angry at him but was intrigued. 'What does he want?' I asked myself. He called, we spoke and caught up, and we rekindled our friendship. He talked about giving it another go, but I was hesitant and still confused at what happened to stop our progress in the first instance. I was happy with the way things were, but at the back of my mind, I did not rule out reconciliation down the line.

Nine months had passed. We still spoke and went on dates. I would stay over at his occasionally if it was late. He would sleep on his sofa. I knew I should not have done this, but we were friends, I thought, and my will power was strong.

I started working on this project with a group of people. Out of all the group there was one girl with whom I got on better with. For several weeks into the project, we worked closer. One day we were in the gym, discussing how we could promote the project further. She mentioned she had dropped some flyers in her boyfriend's store on the such and such street. Immediately I recognised the street. (It was the same street Mr D's business was on.) I then asked what the name of the business was. She confirmed the name of Mr D's business. My jaw dropped. Before I knew, I blurted out Mr D's name. She looked shocked and asked how I knew Mr D? I regained composure and answered that I knew his family, which was the truth. (It was only yesterday I was speaking to Mr D on the phone. He had found out that I was working on the project and congratulated me, etc.) I continued to ask her how long she was with Mr D. She said three years. This meant he was with her when he was seeing me. The penny dropped.

I had got enough information from her to then tackle Mr D. Even though we weren't together at this time, I still felt betrayed by him and his family. I was angry and upset regardless; after all, he was a liar and a cheat. Even at this point he was still trying to get back together with me, knowing he was already in a relationship and completely unavailable to my needs. I was disappointed in myself for being so naive and open to being trapped in this way. As I mentioned before, I was still open for reconciliation with him, but something was telling me it wasn't the right time.

When I had calmed down and felt more rational, I called him and informed him that I'd just met his girlfriend. He was prepared for my phone call as he knew the walls were closing in on him (when he found out that his girlfriend and I were working together). He claimed he called the previous day to tell me but couldn't. Somewhat spineless? His girlfriend had called him immediately after I left the gym, suspicious of how he knew me. His sustained web of lies was unfolding. His excuses were also self-centred and pathetic. "I didn't know what to do." "I found myself in a situation liking two women." And the one that made me want to throw up, "I really care about you." Blah blah.

This 'wrongun' has made me find it very difficult to trust men, which has unfortunately made it difficult for me to move forward with other guys. I became somewhat cynical about trusting men, and if I am honest, I still am. However, looking back and reflecting on the situation from the start, there were signs. I didn't know or think at the time that he had a double life, but I knew that it/ he wasn't right for me. I had the strength to pull away, then to stay and tolerate his broken promises.

T, 29, London, England

Never Try to Right a Mr Wrong – The Tale of Mr Serial Liar

Me and Mr Wrong met at university, in a lecture. We had spoken on social media before we had even met, but when I went to introduce myself he pretended he had no idea who I was. He later explained this was down to my profile picture not living up to real life expectations. I'll get to that later.

He seemed genuinely interested in me, insisting I do this project with him, or help him with that problem. It made me feel special, that he had singled out me out of everybody to be with him. He wasn't unattractive and there was this cheeky quality about him that was quite irresistible. He made me feel that I was the only one he was interested in and we both shared the same sense of humour and thoughts.

Looking back, there were so many red flags! In hindsight, I should have ended it there and then. Firstly there was the time about a couple of weeks in when he was round at my flat and in the middle of the night I woke up and he wasn't there. Further detective work later revealed he had left to go to another girl's flat because "she was upset about something." First flag. Second time was his reasons for never telling his friends or anybody that we were seeing each other. He wanted to keep it secret. Definite second flag. The last red flag that I can recall with absolute clarity was when he told me that, although my face was pretty, from the neck downwards I needed to work on myself and that I resembled a beached whale (sort of). He was insinuating that the pictures of me that he had looked through hadn't prepared him for what I looked like in real life and that I needed to lose some weight. If ANY guy told me now that I had to lose weight I would punch him in the face! It seemed I was under some sort of spell and I couldn't get out from beneath it.

It was a very unhealthy relationship. We spent too much time together and he started to use me for things. I'd pay for dinner "just this once" or buy food for us, spend money on the cinema etc. and he would never reciprocate. He started to make me feel very unhappy about myself and who I was, however at the same time he would tell me I was an incredible person and that he respected me a lot. In a way, he emotionally manipulated me and knew exactly what to say so I would feel bad about myself. He projected his low self-esteem onto me and that's why I think it was very unhealthy. My friends all tried to tell me he wasn't good for me, and they knew exactly what he was doing but I made excuse after excuse for him, saying he was different when we were alone together, and that he was a good person underneath the not so good exterior. I tried to make right what he was doing wrong to justify the relationship we had. His favourite catchphrase was "Honest babe, don't be so paranoid!"

It should have ended it at this point: I went away on holiday; as far as I knew we were all fine. Anyways, I woke up one morning on holiday to see a few messages from friends expressing their disbelief that I had put our relationship on Facebook. Knowing that I hadn't.

I saw his relationship status had changed and it now said 'in a relationship'. It had lots of comments, people applauding him saying how happy they were. I remember messaging one friend back saying simply, "That isn't with me. It's with someone else. It's not me." I was in shock, and then shock turned to anger. I was humiliated that he had done this to me, especially to have gone as far as putting it on Facebook where he knew I would see and find out at the same time as everyone else. There was no respect and there was definitely no remorse. He was too cowardly to even give me a straight answer other than, "You always knew I still loved her (his ex) you know we (me and him) were never in a real relationship so you have to understand, you're a great person but I love her." Don't get me wrong, I did understand to an extent, but going behind my back and then making me look like an idiot? No way! And after a strongly worded text I deleted him out of my life, unfortunately not forever.

Fast forward a few weeks, back to uni life. I spy him in the same bar as me with his girlfriend. I get talking to a guy. I am leaving with said guy when my phone pings. 'Don't do it', it says. It was him! He was controlling me even when I wasn't with him. Safe to say I ignored it and carried on but when I got to my flat I couldn't stop crying. How dare he turn up with her and then try to control what I do and who I see?

Over the next couple of weeks, things didn't work out for him and he attempted to worm his way back to me with apologies and explanations of how he couldn't understand why he left me in the first place. I wish I could say I told him where to go but I was surprised then at how things changed. He became very loving, told people we were together and didn't mind holding my hand in public (he had before!) But before too long I opened my eyes, read his texts/ Facebook messages (on advice from a girlfriend who had seen him in action in a club one night) to and from many other women (mostly about unnamed things) and decided enough was enough. He begged me and begged me to take him back, promised things would be different, said how much he missed me. He started to guilt trip me when he found out I was seeing somebody else. Turns out he had been also seeing someone else for at least a month whilst he was pleading for me to take him back. Once a cheat, always a cheat. I have never believed in that saying more than I do today.

I learned a great deal about the differences between love and lust. Although I may have thought I was in love with him, really I just lusted after what I hoped we would have and faithfully stuck by it even though it was obvious we didn't. I also learned never to allow a man to make me feel worthless or insecure about my appearance, especially in regards to weight. I am who I am, and you shouldn't have to change yourself for anybody.

I didn't just walk out of this relationship with my head held high, knowing my Mr Right was out there. I was very scarred. It took my current boyfriend many months to gain my trust, I was extremely paranoid and I remember one time he hadn't returned to his home by 4am and I convinced myself he had gone off with somebody else. By the time he did get back I was a wreck and didn't know what to do. However, my boyfriend dealt with my problems with kindness and patience and that's how I gradually learned to trust him and the reason we are still together three years later. Being with him is such a difference from what I had previously; I still can't quite believe I got this lucky. There is no jealousy, no lies and no secrets. Although we don't live in the same city, I know there is no issue of him cheating on me. The most significant thing is that we are always on the same page, and he treats me like a princess, although half the time I am completely undeserving of it!

This is the most important message I can give: If he tells you "You'll never find anyone better than me", you will. There are probably ten times more men who are better than he is. Don't change yourself or your appearance for anyone; I promise there is someone out there who will love you, respect you and who will eat cupcakes and junk with you, and not like you just for the number on your waistband.

Just never try to right a Mr Wrong.

Rachel Thomas, 24, London, England

The Year of the Rat

I met Lee in 2008 . The year of the rat. He was a smooth, caramel-skinned brother with the widest smile I ever saw. His skin was as silky smooth as his words, and his eyes as piercing as his lies.

I met Lee at a bar. I was 21 years old and wide-eyed. He'd offered me a drink, which I accepted. He'd said he was 23 and a fitness instructor at a nearby Virgin Active fitness centre. He had a body to die for and charm to boot. I was whisked off my feet and hung onto every word he said as he entertained me with funny stories at his work. We exchanged numbers and began going out.

Lee was a real gentleman, full of compliments and flattery. Although we'd go out to house parties together, we never used to go out much. If we did, I'd seem to end up footing the bill as Lee insisted he hadn't been paid yet. He even went to the ATM only to come back to the dinner table saying the machine had swallowed his card!

"I can't believe it, babe!"

When I asked why he didn't just pay by card, he simply said, "I don't believe in these machines. Can't trust 'em."

Little did I know that it was he who couldn't be trusted!

Three months into our relationship, I get a call from an irate woman screaming down the phone.

"How long have you been seeing my man!!"

I suddenly felt like I was on the set of Eastenders as she continued her torrent of abuse at me. I found out he had met her the same night and had been dating us both since.

Of course this Serial Liar had to be shown the door, but not before a serious dressing down from me. The absolute joke of it all was he actually told me I was the one in the wrong and that the woman had obviously got the wrong number (either that or she was deranged). He stood there staring me blank in the face, telling me I had trust issues and needed to face my insecurities!

I was convinced I was going to get to the bottom of this, so I rang Sheena (we'd at this point become allies) and suggested we both go down to Virgin Active and pay him a little surprise visit. She paused for what seemed like an eternity before saying, "He doesn't work at Virgin. He works at Dixons."

It was then I realised that this man had been spinning a web of lies around us both about absolutely everything, and we were the poor, unsuspecting party. I was livid. To satisfy my curiosity, I rang both Virgin Active and Dixons only to find out that he worked at neither.

Wanting to find out what else he'd lie about—yes, I admit I went deeeep—I did some detective work on ancestry.com, only to find out that he wasn't, in fact, 23 as he had said, but was 33 and lived at home with his mum. In addition to that, he was not born in Jamaica as he'd previously boasted but, in actual fact, in West Hampstead, and his middle name was, in fact, Abiola—not very Caribbean to me!!

I can't say for sure, but I suspect he was unemployed. What I am sure of is his full-time voluntary job as a Serial Liar left him redundant!

Michelle, 27, Tottenham, England, England

Letting Go of Mr Serial Liar

The running theme to these stories is that each of these men left their woman feeling disempowered. By shutting them away from the truth, these men took away the woman's right to choose. They grossly misled these women into thinking they were offering something that, in fact, could never be. They made these women believe that they were or would be offering them a secure, happy, monogamous relationship. This gross act of lying is a sign of nothing more than cowardice and control. It shows lack of courage to come clean or be honest with one, either, or both parties and a very unattractive desire for control and manipulation. By lying to these women, these men are under the false impression that they are 'running the game,' 'having their cake and eating it' by weakening and deceiving their 'partners.' (I use the term loosely!) Do not expect them to see or acknowledge your pain because men like this are concerned with only one thing. Themselves. Don't expect a clear or coherent explanation for this man's actions as there isn't one. He simply lied so that he could have whatever he wanted at little or no cost. Their lack of respect for you needs no explaining. The explaining is all in the actions. They are liars and will do whatever it takes to continue the lie until it is too late.

Sadly for them, they do not realise that at some point their lies will be discovered and that karma will come back around. **Note to women:** karma should not come in the form of revenge but in the form of forgiveness and letting go. There is no need to scratch cars or behave like a crazy woman scorned. Let go of Mr Serial Liar; go and get on with your life. Seek happiness. Mr Serial Liar has created his own karma as somebody who feels the need to lie, deceive, and control others cannot achieve true happiness because inside they are very unhappy souls indeed. At some point they will have to discover and unravel the root of their unhappiness, anger, and need to control. Their problem not yours. We may believe that they are roaming the Earth feeling as light as a feather as they lie their way through marriages, relationships, and life, getting away scot-free. But we must remember that, just as we have our inklings, urges, and intuition, so do others, and they will be dealt with accordingly. To Mr Serial Liar, lying is an addiction, a first port of call, but remember, ladies, revenge should not come in the form of calling his wife and screaming obscenities down the phone, breaking up families, or letting down tyres, but by removing yourself from the situation and seeking your own happiness. People who are happy attract happiness. People who are unhappy attract even more unhappiness. The End.

Why Do People Lie?

People lie for many different reasons. Everyone at some stage or another has told a little white lie to get out of trouble or to protect another's feeling. For example, "Do you like the colour of this new dress I've bought?" "Yes, darling it's lovely." Whether these white lies are needed or not, I'm sure there is not a single person reading this book who has not told one.

'Serial Liar' is my own term for someone who lies repeatedly however the official terms for liars are Impulsive Liars, Compulsive Liars and Pathological Liars. Here, I will explain the differences.

People lie often to paint a picture of one who has a much more 'colourful' life than they actually have. These types of liars are known as **Impulsive Liars.** They often lie about the smallest of things, such as where they went out on the weekend or how ill they were when, in actual reality, they lay on the couch all weekend watching TV instead of painting the town red or were in bed with the flu instead of having to be wheeled down to A & E with 'meningitis-type' symptoms. Impulsive Liars often lie to embellish or exaggerate the truth to make their lives and themselves sound more interesting than they actually are or to gain a greater reaction. For example, a sense of awesomeness: "Wow! You shook hands with Samuel L Jackson on a night out. Megan Fox blew you a kiss at her premiere!" Or a sense of great sympathy: "Oh gosh, wow you've been through a lot. A near-death experience and you made it through. Oh perish the thought of it being any worse. Well done you, for surviving that one! Rest up!" This sense of popularity and interest the lie has attracted is just the magnetism Mr Serial Liar often uses to hook his victim. Not always—but often. Impulsive Liars are often not even aware they are lying. It is simply a default mode they slip into or revert to in order to paint a picture of who they would like to be. Impulsive Liars do not think about the consequences of their actions, only the embellishment of the lie. Impulsive Liars often have a low sense of self-esteem and an increasing desire or need for validation and attention as well as a desire to take centre stage in the lives of others.

Compulsive Liars also act on impulse. They lie also to embellish and exaggerate mundane activities but also to manipulate and control others. Compulsive Liars do not feel any remorse or regret for their actions and will happily repeat the same lie over and over again with not a thought for the consequences. To Compulsive Liars, lying is second nature. Lying is a habitual routine that makes them feel safe. Telling the truth does not come naturally. Telling the truth feels awkward. Compulsive Liars often lie for personal gain and self-interest and are often controlling and manipulative. They suffer from a diminished sense of accountability and responsibility, and it is never their fault. Blame and shame are often placed upon their partner for not being "XYZ enough" or "not having done XYZ."

The difference between Compulsive and **Pathological Liars** is that Compulsive Liars know the difference between a truth and a lie and a Pathological Liar does not. Whatever the 'type' of liar, the person needs to seek professional help to create a change within.

Quiz Time!

Can You Spot a Serial Liar?

When a person is lying the evidence can usually be found in:

a) Type of words that are used

b) Non-verbal expression

c) Pitch and tone of voice

The addition of an epilogue when recounting events is a sign of:

a) A true story

b) A false story

c) Both

A person who is lying often recounts a story:

a) Starting from the end and ending with beginning

b) No sequential order

c) Using strict chronological order

A false smile uses:

a) All the muscles in the face

b) Only the muscle around the eyes

c) Only the muscles around the mouth

When recounting information liar will:

a) Use limited hand gestures

b) Over exaggerate hand gestures

c) Sit on their hands

When lying a liar will often touch:

a) Chest, arms, hands

b) Face, mouth, throat

c) Legs, feet and ankles

A common gesture for a liar is:

a) Interlocking hands behind their head

b) Scratching their nose or ea

c) Nodding incessantly

When liar's story will:

a) Contain lots of emotion

b) Lack emotion

c) Contain lots of detail

Liars commonly leave out words like:

a) Pronouns- I, me, my

b) Adjectives- describing words like beautiful, amazing, exhilarating

c) Adverbs- slowly, happily, excitedly

A real smile uses:

a) Lower half of face

b) The muscles around the mouth area

c) All the muscles in the face

Answers on page
287

Chapter 6: Emotionally Unavailable Men

The Mr Wrongs we have come across so far have all got one thing in common. These men are Emotionally Unavailable. What exactly does Emotionally Unavailable mean? The term "emotionally unavailable" usually refers to those who create barriers between themselves and others in an effort to avoid emotional intimacy.

These kinds of relationships can be very taxing and painful for the person involved with the E.U.M. (Emotionally Unavailable Man). An E.U.M. often leaves their partner feeling very confused, distressed, unloved, and neglected, and they end up continually wondering whether they are in a relationship at all. The more you try to seek love from the E.U.M., the further and further apart you become as he will begin to create distance within the relationship. Relationships with an E.U.M. is like two magnets continually repelling and attracting but never actually coming together for enough time to create a bond that is meaningful. Women involved with an E.U.M. often blame themselves for not being enough or for not being worthy of being loved. These men proved a "Hook a Duck" and "10p Slot Machine" type of relationship that never really takes off or progresses. 'Commitment' and 'attachment' are enemies to the E.U.M, and if you ask for it or make him feel as though he needs it, then you secretly become an enemy too.

What causes E.U.M.?

Let's face it: men are not typically wired to be overly emotional. They are wired to be practical and logical, to think rationally and provide solutions. Women are more emotional in their responses and intuitive in their reactions. Yes, there are exceptions, but I'm talking generally here. I don't want a man to cry with me whilst watching an emotional film; I want a man to pass me the tissues. In saying this, everyone needs to feel love and affection from their partner, a sense of connection and intimacy. These men are unable to provide us with these things for many reasons, such as:

- Unresolved childhood issues relating to attachment

- The belief that if they demonstrate loving emotions they are somehow weak

- Fear of commitment

- Feelings of unworthiness or inadequacy

- Unresolved relationship issues

- They are already attached or married

There is nothing to say that these men are bad or villains in anyway, but everything about this list shouts "BEWARE!" You will never be able to "fix" a person or change them into the person you want them to be. We must be completely whole and happy within ourselves before we can provide a stable and loving relationship to someone else. Why live with a Commitmentphobe when you need and want stability and commitment? Let Mr E.U.M. address his own issues before reeling you in for a game of push and pull. Relationships with an E.U.M. will bring only heartbreak and pain until he tackles the issues.

Mr Unavailable

I met him at work. When we spoke, my heart raced. I loved his stories. I believed he could complete me. We'd worked together for a while, and when I left the team, we finally hooked up. We both told each other that we'd liked each other for ages. We both confided that we were crap at relationships. (He told me about how he'd had a girlfriend at Uni who was beautiful and he was besotted, but she was a bitch to him. He'd been a sucker and she'd walked all over him. They'd brought the worst sides out in each other. Since then, he wouldn't tolerate bitches. I wasn't sure whether he was warning me, which felt odd. (I should have seen it as a warning sign.) But I wasn't a bitch, so I didn't take too much notice of it.) He told me he wanted this to work and that I should tell him if he was annoying. I told him I could be neurotic at times. (I often go for a bit of gentle self-deprecation when others are opening up.) But I explained that it was nothing to worry about—I think he clung to this throw-away comment until the day we split up.

In my head, I had no doubt it would work out. How could it not? We had fun. We got each other. I thought we were a match.

One night we were all out in a group. He and his mates hailed a cab. I lived close by. Could he walk me to the top of the road? It was 2 a.m. I was on my own. He could get a cab from there. He brushed me off and jumped in the cab. The seed of doubt was sown. I noticed little things—red flags—but I guess I didn't want to acknowledge them or believe them to be warning signs because I liked him so much. For example: he texted late at night and took hours to respond to messages; we met up at the end of the evening and he was generally tired from everything else he'd done that week; his week's schedule was packed; he saw me when he was free. When I suggested things, he was always busy. I didn't understand.

This relationship was based on a friendship, and he'd told me we could trust each other—yes, you guessed it—before we first slept together! So why was he playing games and being so aloof? He didn't do anything wrong, no dramas, no cheating. It just didn't feel right. I didn't feel confident. I didn't trust him. How much of this was him or me, I still don't know. I kept remembering what he'd said, 'I really want this to work. If I'm annoying, tell me.' It repeated in my head every time he brushed off one of my suggestions to do something: the cinema, a trip away, an evening I was free next week. ... Now, I was confused.

We met up. We had quite a nice evening. I went back to his. He fell asleep. No sex, no chat. I felt neglected. I woke him. I felt that impulse. That surge. I needed to know that he cared. That he was bothered. It turned out he wasn't. He asked me why girls always talk about their issues at 1 a.m. Why they were so stressful. Why they asked so many questions. He didn't pull me close and tell me not to worry. He needed to chill out. Not to feel pressurised. This was how he was. He was taking things slow. He wasn't going to change. I didn't want this guy to change. This was the one man I'd met whom I liked just as he was. He was confused. I'd asked the question, highlighted that things weren't running to plan. I'd let him know I was vulnerable. The damage had been done. He was busy. He needed to think. We met up a week or two later (after radio silence and a cancelled arrangement). He was still confused and hung over—nice! "We should be patient with each other," I said.

"That's not an option," I was told.

Eventually I told him we should forget things. I didn't even try to convince him. Not really. He didn't fight to save the relationship he'd wanted weeks before and had waited for for months as he originally implied. He let me do the breaking up. I was told by a friend who knew his ex that he was a commitment-phobe, that after a romantic first few months he called time out. As we parted on the day we broke up, he said he was sorry. I knew then this was what he wanted all along, despite not ever saying it straight out.

I called him later. I told him that if he wanted things to end, he should have told me and not been a coward. Eventually he did (although he seemed more concerned that I'd called him a coward than anything else). He said he couldn't give me what I wanted and that we wanted different things. He spoke about girls again—previous relationships. Girls wanting to see him too often. The last girl he'd dated, who I have been told by a mutual friend was actually a really nice girl, had wanted to spend time with him when all he wanted was to go to sleep at 10 p.m. every now and again. Girls to him were a nuisance—I was one of those girls now.

I was on the list of crazy women who wanted too much. I wasn't the girl whom he'd known, his friend or the person in whom he once saw potential. I was something that would wrench him from his friends, demand his time, and put him under pressure. (I note here that I'm actually a busy girl myself with a lovely group of friends and sense of independence.) I went in on myself. Blamed myself. Tortured myself. Six months of crying and thinking that I'd screwed it all up by being ... you guessed it—neurotic! If I hadn't had been so demanding ... If I had just left it ... If only I hadn't told him I was upset ... I had no confidence.

Six months on, I heard that Mr Unavailable, Mr 'Take-It-Slow-You-Crazy- Woman,' had jetted off on impulse to India with a girl he'd just met. Finally, I felt vindicated, although as my friends told me a 100 times over, I should have realised this for myself. It shouldn't have been about him, but it was. Finally, Mr Take-It-Slow had taken it fast and proved to me that what I'd wanted was never unreasonable (a walk home at night, a text, a call to see how I was doing). He was going to India! I only suggested the cinema!!! With me, he had embarked on something he couldn't commit to and blamed me (and women-kind) on his way out. 'Bye-bye crazy lady.'

Maybe he will commit to this new girl; maybe he won't. What I've learnt is that you should never let someone make you think that wanting to be cared for is unreasonable, neurotic, or an annoying female trait. I am not a girl like the rest; I am me. And the rest, well, they are unique too. Never let a man's fear of a relationship or issues with his past experiences and relationships make you feel like the failure. Know what you want and believe in your worth.

Allison, 31, Suffolk, England,

Mr Big

I once dated this guy; I'll call him "Mr. Big." I don't even know if you would call it "dating," but I'll share the story and let you be the judge. We'd known one another for a little over a year, and Mr. Big wanted to jump my bones, but I ran from him like the plague. Why? you ask. Well, I was already extremely intrigued by him. But because of where we met, I felt all he wanted was to taste my honey, and I was ready for a relationship, so I knew getting all hot and sweaty with him would lead to trouble. We hung out from time to time and had conversations, but we were never physical.

He accused me of being scared that he would wear me out. Naturally THAT wasn't what I was worried about, so I eventually told him I was running because I wanted a relationship, but I felt all he wanted was my hot and juicy. He said he wasn't looking for a relationship, but if one happened, he wasn't opposed to it. Having been a game player, I knew this was just something men said to get in the honey pot. I told him, "Yeah, OK, well I'm not ready to take that risk."

Time passed and I dealt with The DOC, The Filler, Mr Dreamer, and My RoD (different men for different stories!), all in no particular order. After surviving that, I figured I'd have nothing to lose. So after one of my gatherings where Mr. Big was in attendance, I told him I was ready. I told him that I understood he was not looking for a relationship and that I was cool with that. He fought me at first, saying he didn't want to be a fall-back guy. I assured him he wasn't that because I always wanted him, but I was just not ready to set myself up for heartbreak. Again, he said although he was not looking for a relationship, if it happened, he was not against it. He just had some things he was focused on that were more important.

We got BUSY and OMG the man was MORE than a beast! He did things I had never experienced before. This way, that way, and every other way; he had me feeling like I was going to convulse and pass out! He said he didn't want to "share the honey pot," so I made it clear that I didn't do distance. He assured me he would close the distance and that he was going to "spoil the honey pot" and he surely did. I told him I could see why he had so many women chasing him. He threw out that line that everyone didn't get everything I got. *eyebrow raised* Yeah, OK! Because of where we stood, I never asked questions about his life. No, "Where are you going? When are you coming back? Who's with you?" Nothing. All I ever asked was to see him if it had been too long.

We continued our "sessions," spending the night with one another, going out together alone, with our children, with my friends, and he even attended family functions at my house. He told me he loved me all the while maintaining that we were NOT in a relationship.

I said to him that although I wanted more, I knew that I was just the next chic to him, but that I respected that he was not ready for a relationship, that he was single, and that I was willing to be patient and continue as we were because his character was showing he was well worth the wait. He said I was NOT just the next chic (yeah, whatever!), but hell, no other man around at the time had his credentials and character, so I wasn't losing anything by hanging in there. It was actually giving us time to experience things and get to know one another to see if we, in fact, could be more than FWB. (That's how I saw us; he never agreed.)

Life-changing events happened that seemed to bring us closer. For a short while we didn't get to see one another as much, but we stayed in contact. Once we did see each other, it was GREAT! There was no sex involved, but the emotion was there. When things got back to normal, once again he ROCKED MY WORLD! Good gosh, that man could go. Anyway, out of nowhere, he all of a sudden got distant. We would speak, but he stayed away and eventually his conversation got scarce. I asked what was up with the distance, and he eventually said that he felt I was trying to turn him into a "do boy" and change him into who I wanted him to be, that I was trying to force him into a relationship, and that I lived my life for my friends. This floored me and let me see that if he really believed these things, he didn't really know me very well at all. Whether he was being real with his explanation or not only he knows, but I had to accept it and move on.

We're still cool and speak from time to time, but it sure ain't what it used to be. So where we once referred to one another as friends, I now believe, as patient as he was, it was all about him getting sex, and we were never more that. FWB.

Lady-J, 39, KCMO, USA

Attachment Hell

I met Andrew at Uni in 2004. I was in my second year. He was my flatmate's friend. He'd called her once and heard me in the background. We clicked from the get-go, and we ended up talking on her phone for three hours. It was full of innuendo and sexual banter—what I would call tongue-in-cheek cheeky banter.

Three weeks later he came down to Manchester, where I was at Uni, for a weekend. From the beginning we were slightly wary of each other, but that night he stayed in my bed and we had sex. From the beginning it was quite clear that he fancied me. The next day I had work. My friend told me that he had really missed me throughout the day and even described him as a "sad puppy dog".

We continued talking on the phone for hours after that, and three weeks later we decided we should go away together. I organised everything. I worried about beds and money. I was wanted us to have single beds and was wary about paying for everything on my credit card whilst he wanted a dirty weekend and was happy to pay me back when the time came. I think we clashed in terms of vision as to how the relationship would work out. I cancelled the weekend.

Even though we get on really well—we laugh at the same things—we think very differently. We would argue about perceptions of a relationship. I felt he was all about the physical but I wanted to be reassured that we would be a couple and do things together. He talked the talk amazingly well. He said that sex was the basis of an intimate relationship. He made constant excuses as to why we shouldn't meet up. I offered for us to go to a theme park together, to meet up with friends, and he made countless excuses, mainly saying he wasn't keen until we'd had sex. "It cemented the relationship. The foundation is sex, and from there we grow as a couple." We both eventually agreed we were coming from different perspectives.

Despite our different ideals, we stayed in constant contact, and we began to depend on each other. Andrew was quite a negative person. He would find a negative in everything, and strangely I found that quite fascinating. It drew me to him. However, his negativity began to affect me and I became wary.

Andrew and I were out of contact for a year, and I was going through a rocky patch with my then-boyfriend when he boomeranged back into my life. He tried to get information out of me about my boyfriend, asking me why we weren't getting on and telling me I deserved better. I eventually broke up with my boyfriend, and Andrew became my confidante. It felt like we were going out. He was always staying at my place. We had a full-blown sexual relationship. He'd meet me after work, call me all the time; however, five months down the line he was adamant that he was not my boyfriend. He had no interest in calling me his girlfriend, nor did he want to meet my family. He was adopted as a child and had a very negative view of family, and at this period in his life, he was on a quest to find his mum.

2006 was the crux point. Although we were now deemed 'boyfriend' and 'girlfriend,' we were constantly fighting. We would have a killer argument, break up, then make up, then have amazing sex. We fell into that unhealthy pattern. It was hard to let go. He was always the person who would support me and be there for me. What bothered me was that he never wanted to do things with me, like go to the theatre. Again he made countless excuses as to why we couldn't go; however, a year later I found out that he had been declared bankrupt.

This was the year that I found out the extent of his lies. I knew he loved me, but he would constantly lie about things. He lied about things he had achieved, places he'd been, even about the fact he had a car! Was he trying to impress me? Shield me? If only he'd realised that he didn't need to be like that. If he had just been honest about his dreams and aspirations, I wouldn't have had such high expectations. Things began to come together at this point. Andrew had lied to me about his name when we first met. Three years later, I still didn't know how old Andrew was, his full name, and his date of birth.

He hid bits of information from me. He ever did anything official. He would never sign up to the doctors or anything like that. When I look back, I was so naive and young. He had serious attachment issues. He could never really offer me a loving, honest, healthy relationship, yet he didn't want me to be with anyone else. Whilst he was possessive over me, he never wanted to do anything with me that would cement him as a person in my life. I think these issues stemmed from being adopted and feeling abandoned, but I couldn't fix him. Because of his issues, he didn't "want" to be a real person in my life. I decided I needed to have a cut-off. I knew I couldn't have this person in mine.

It was hard, and I had to place a division there by telling myself I did not care. The next few years he bobbed in and out of my life. Sometimes we were on; sometimes we were off, but by this time I'd stopped telling him things. He lies a lot, so I found myself starting to do the same thing. At the start of our relationship, he would really "big me up" and make me feel like I was the most important woman in the world. However, it was now 2007 and as we became closer, I started digging deeper, and by this time he began to put me down a lot. He would make references to the way I looked; he would make comments about me in front of others, such as, "You can't really cook, can you?" I remember watching the TV with him once when he said, "That girl on TV is quiet ugly. She looks like you though." I was shocked at first and really didn't know how to respond, but after a while, I too became horrible. His nasty comments began to sharpen my claws, and I too became a b**ch. I remember once we were being intimate, and he covered my face with my hair, as if he didn't want to look at me. Looking back, perhaps this was a reflection of his own self-hatred and inability to connect with a human being.

It got so bad, but still I couldn't let go of Andrew. Things took a real turn for the worse when Andrew's friend came to stay at my house. We'd all been out, and we began discussing pro-abortion. The next night Andrew woke me up at 11 p.m. to tell me he wasn't happy with my views about pro-abortion. He said, "I hate women who think they can just get rid of a baby whenever they want. I hate people like you." I started to cry. He kept calling me "off-key." He made me question myself, my beliefs, who I was. I told him that I didn't need him in my life, that this was my house, and I questioned exactly what it was that he was bringing to the table. He replied, "No you **do** need me. No one will have you."

The inference was that I needed to change my views in order to be a better human being. He made me question everything. I suggested couple counselling, but he insisted that it me who was the mad one.

I wish I had been strong enough to leave then, but the tipping point was when I eventually allowed this relationship to transform me from a young innocent girl to a woman who was now bitter, angry, and insane. I'd put on a bit of weight with Andrew as he used to feed me a lot. He would pile mountains of food on my plate. I thought he was just a loving boyfriend who just wanted me to be happy. I'd always eat it and be satisfied. One day I asked Andrew why he overloaded my plate with food. He simply replied, "I overload your plate full of food to see if you can finish your food or see if you have the self-discipline to know your plate." When I looked at this, this was a metaphor for our relationship. He had been testing my boundaries, seeing how much I could handle, and scorning me *every time I accepted his bad treatment of me. We had a massive argument. He drove me insane and I threatened him with violence. It's not something I'm proud of and deeply regret. The police were called by a nearby neighbour. It took this to wake me up and make me realise that this situation, this man was no good for me.*

Looking back I can see how I allowed this man to infiltrate my life time and time again. He would appear then reappear into my life, gain confidential information from me about past boyfriends, then throw it back in my face. I would dread asking him to social events. (We've only been to four.) I didn't want my friends to put him down or feel that I had to defend him. They were sick of hearing about the pain and distress he was putting me through. I began to ostracise myself from my friends as he would always call and see where I was then demand a time that I would be home so that he could call me. I began to feel that my friends were interrupting my timetable with Andrew. He made out that friends and family were not important to him and so should not be important to me. I ostracised myself in the hope that we would one day have a beautiful, healthy relationship at the cost of my self-worth, my friends, and my sanity.

Ann Marie, 29, London, England

I'm Guilty on Three Counts

"Hey why didn't you call me last night? It's the same story with you over and over again," she'd say, listening to Eric's feeble excuses with frustration yet still anticipating a valid answer to keep their affair going. On this occasion he never sweet talked his way out of this dispute, knowing that she would always be there, his little Angel— loving, caring, and too forgiving. With no attempt to appease her, in

his arrogance he brushed off her anguish and her attempts to analyse his failure to communicate. At the end of the call, infuriated at his shoddy effort of a relationship, she wondered why she couldn't cut her ties with this heartthrob. Perhaps because Eric gazed too often into her eyes, souls meeting, understanding each other as he held her hands, whispering words of passion and promises of better days to come. In his awe he studied every facet of her face, pet named her, and caressed her hair and hands in every meet. It could never be a facade. She felt his chi, the most powerful of love energies, when they met for lunch encounters.

"Ang, I could do anything for you. I am so crazy about you." Eric admitted he was smitten.

In such a short space of time, before their third date, Eric Andre had declared in song "Don't Wanna Be a Player No More." He was full of songs. His long-term relationship had drawn to a close, and his numerous women friends and potential partners were no longer enticing now that he had started seeing Ang.

"What have you done to my friend? He is head over heels in love!" his friend would say, reiterating Eric's words. Ang was never one to be easily convinced, but listening to Eric's friend was assuring. He recognised and confirmed what Ang already could feel; Eric had found "The One".

He had opened up to his new love and spilt his innermost secrets, never ever told before. Both besotted, they would tell each other how the other frequented their dreams sequentially. They had connected deeply and were ready to take the relationship to another level, only there was a major barrier.

Her.

In each attempt Ang tried to hear about the other woman, the unrelenting woman who causes misery, the insignificant woman as she had been portrayed, still she remained in darkness. Ang should either walk away or take her chances and trust in Eric's word, believing that she now ruled his world and it was time to plan their future. He had said the other woman was the past and Ang was the prospect of happiness, prosperity, and family....

It had been months of marvellous meetings, followed by his avoidance from broken promises, then the reconciliation; this pattern was repetitive. By now she was hooked, despite being a walking skeleton, frail and subject to ailments due to her obsession with loving Eric. She must have enjoyed the emotional turmoil because with every opportunity she had to put an end to this when she had felt rejected, she continuously went back to replay her catch phrase, "Why haven't you called?" Eric would have known that the parrot would soon ring again, asking another similar question, still perched in the same position, unable to spread her wings and free herself from the entrapments of this cage.

Then she got over him. She had forgotten about him for a few days or weeks at a time. Miraculously, she had taken a few steps forward. She was healthy, happy, and the vibrant thing she had always been. Regaining her life, her visions were clearer and her pathway was steady—until the trigger, his voice, his humour, his photos and paraphernalia had taken her several steps backwards. Just one more time, one more chance to play with him, to listen to his stories and assurances of their future, to hear how she is the most wonderful and special woman and more, so she must have desired to ask in the coming days, "Why have you been avoiding me?" It was only a matter of time before her favourite questions were asked.

And she waited patiently and tolerantly for his complete closure with the lady of his past, waiting to hear this woman's wrongdoings, to hear another tale of how this obsessive, lesser woman won't leave him alone. Like an avid audience, she waited to hear and see more drama, waiting for the happy ending, the absolute dissolution of their relationship so that she could take her trophy home.

Ang had become far from an Angel, fallen from grace to compete with another woman. Even though it was not her style, she had wanted to win the race. But in her heart of hearts, she pitied his obsessive woman who monitored and tracked him with telephone calls in almost every one of their dates. It was true this woman was not letting go, no matter if Eric said he was moving on or how he had hurt her previously. Moreover, it was also true that Ang was impersonating this behaviour. Hadn't she too been long suffering, trying to establish a sincere present relationship, craving that he would be a one-woman man and in so doing cutting off his ex-relationships and dedicating himself to her? In her heart she pitied herself more now than the other woman.

She knew that it was the wrong idea to fight over him as he would have wanted, the wrong idea to continue holding on to nothing but a flaky relationship and to continue in the wrong direction. She knew that he was not worthy to take any more of her, for he had benefited from her abundance of love and her kind thoughts and actions for his well-being. He had already in his clutches her heart, her mind, and it would be wrong too if he owned her body.

Epilogue

Lessons to learn in life and love, and I learnt the hard way with no one but myself to blame. It took some time before I could admit that I was the one with the wrong idea. Yes, I had been lied to initially, but from the onset, if I listened and truly listened, not only to the words of Mr Eric Wrong but to my inner voice, I would have known that I was walking along the wrong path.

So how did I inflict self-harm all in the name of love?

I am guilty on three counts:

Count One—and listen up ladies who may be in the same boat, it gets turbulent. He tells you that his relationship is on the rocks or over, they are going their separate ways, she is negligent in his affairs, and he is unhappy. I (you) believe him, having faith in his words that you are there at the right time to save the day, you are the wonder woman he has been waiting for all his life, you are the wife. So here we have the ideology of the competitive theory, believing and swallowing his account that they are history or heading for a termination and you are his permanent destination. She is the ex, and you are lucky to be next. The other woman hasn't got the qualities you have; maybe you are prettier, more petite or taller than, lighter or darker, fuller or slimmer, brighter or more intelligent; simply said, you think you must be better than her. Well, I must have bought that story. Although I don't agree with rivalry, somehow I believed that I am the one who will make Mr E. A Wrong happy and save him from the misery of the inferior woman.

Count Two, you see that he is Mr 360 degree, head turning on the street when he passes another woman—any woman—taller, shorter, fatter, or thinner. You notice this trait from the very first date, but you dismiss it. He is only looking, even though he has been focused in that direction for more than five minutes and has started to smile, and not with you. What's wrong with him admiring other women? you say. Two can play. You copy the game and he says "no way". So after our romantic meal on the first date, the relationship blues revealed its true colours. But brush it off because you want to be in love, and you sulk as you notice his serial flirting tendencies each and every time you are out.

Count three and failing rule number one. I was guilty of playing to the name Angel, unconditional loving shown towards him without even considering how I need to love me. How did I continue to love a man who dishonours me in count two? I hated that behaviour, so why didn't I wave him good-bye rather than to feel insecure and turn a blind eye with pain in my gut and desperate to cry? Other than the flirtatious behaviours and lack of communication at times, the greatest offense was his broken promises, which he never showed the slightest remorse for. After one or two of these incidents, surely it should have been enough to call it a day, but no, I was a glutton for punishment. It was torture, hoping for more from him and giving more of my heart and feeling like it was bleeding. I was destroying my anatomy: my heart, my mind, under-nourishing my stomach, and crushing my spirit. Maybe I truly wanted to die, to transcend to another realm and live up to being his Angel. The bottom line is the number one rule is to love oneself, as loving a man more than yourself is the wrong idea.

Amanda Epe, London, England

Top Ten Signs You Are Dating an E.U.M.

Physically Unavailable

Emotionally Unavailable Men are not just emotionally unavailable, they are physically unavailable too. Pinning this man down is like a challenging quest to contact aliens in outer space. He may text and call whenever it suits him, but he is never around when you need him. This man will never help you with things that are important to you, such as moving, birthdays, weddings, and funerals. He will rarely attend social events with you as this will only confirm that you are indeed a committed couple. Perish the thought!

James Bond Air of Mystery

This man desperately wants to be some sort of hero in your life that you can't live without, yet he never really reveals enough about himself for you to truly know who he is. He will never share intimate details about himself, such as past history, relationships, childhood, or important events in his life. He prefers to create an air of mystery to keep you guessing and to keep you hooked. This mystery man is one closed book that you do not need to prise open. Leave on the shelf and write your own story!

Secrets and Lies

As demonstrated in Ann Marie's story, this man may lie about his life, his material possessions, financial situation, age, and even his name! His life is a total fabrication constructed upon secrets and lies. This man may be so used to his Pinocchio porkies that he forgets what he's told you. He may get ratty when you begin to question him and make you feel that you are paranoid. Don't let him spin his web of deceit around you and don't question yourself. If something is off, it's off! Trust your intuition. If you smell a rat, then it's probably because you're dating one. Men like this lie to deny themselves of the fact that they are a real human being in a real relationship, or they may even be attached or already married.

Flattery and Cheeky Charm

These men will tell you the sun shines out of your backside. He will compliment your smile, your eyes, and everything about you. These men have silver tongues and are well versed with those silky smooth words. It is easy to be taken in by these words; however, remember they are just that: words. When you start to question his actions is when the real man will surface. The fact that "you have the cutest bum he ever saw" or "eyes as deep as the ocean" will mean nothing once he pulls the curtain and exits offstage.

Intimacy Avoidance

Similar to secrets and lies, these men avoid intimate questions that could lead to a sense of closeness with another. In order to maintain the façade, they must not let anyone in. They build walls and defences like a moat around their castle so that they do not ever appear vulnerable or needy towards another. Letting someone in is dangerous. Their deeply ingrained fear of being attacked or open to humiliation, loss, or even the deepening of a closer emotional bond keeps them closed off to love. While the castle cries out for love, the person in it screams, "Why commit to someone who could eventually abandon me when I could exist happily alone?" Why drown in a murky moat when you could find someone who is open to love, affection, and commitment?

Lack of Commitment

An E.U.M. will never mention the dreaded C-word. The C-word is the fear of all fears, danger of all dangers. The C-word will bring pain and grief and an end to all happiness. The C-word equals the dreaded COMMITMENT. Committing to another is like signing your life away. Who wants to be ball and chained when you can run free? Commitmentphobes fear commitments of all sorts: commitment to a plan, commitment to decisions, commitment to keeping promises, and commitment to a person. Committing to someone or something means that a decision has to be made, reached and adhered too. Sticking at something means that there is no way out, no room for manoeuvre. We may now be forever at the mercy of the commitment we have made. This is the mother of all fears. How do I know I want strawberry jam when I haven't tasted the raspberry yet? These men are Commitmentphobes due to their negative beliefs about love, relationships, and commitment. The Commitmentphobe may display signs of wanting a relationship, but once the honeymoon phase is over and the rose-tinted glasses have been taken off, the running shoes come on. The grass is always greener with a Commitmentphobe, yet they fail to realise that the reason the grass fades is because they are walking all over it!

Conversely, Commitmentphobes can be quite loving and affectionate, but this is because they know the relationship isn't going to last. This is in line with their 'live fast, die young' attitude. Commitmentphobes tend not to have stable jobs or stable lives because they fear making any kind of stable decision as it suggests longevity.

Severe Commitmentphobes may actually love the woman they are with and fight hard to win her over. However, when he eventually gets the woman of his dreams, he can never commit to staying—yet at the same time is unable to walk away completely. The woman is left feeling totally and utterly confused and may feel she is going insane. I can assure you, you are not. Whilst you may love Mr Commitmentphobe and he you, will he ever be able to provide you with the security and stability your relationship needs?

Unreliability

In line with the E.U.M.'s actions, they are completely unreliable. You can never count on these men for anything. They may promise to call or pick you up and then forget or find something more important to do. He does things according to his schedule, not yours or 'ours.' He is often late to meet you or cancels plans and dates you have arranged. E.U.M.s are often unreliable because of their fear of commitment or fear of becoming too close, or perhaps he has plans with his wife!

Wants to Get Physical Far Too Quickly

Sex is often the basis of the relationship. They may convince you that you belong together and that sex will cement the relationship or that it is more important than other aspects. Don't get me wrong—the sex may be undeniably good but will more likely last as long as the relationship! Sex is a physical act rather than an emotionally intimate one in these cases. Think Daniel Cleaver in Bridget Jones and his desperate escape in the morning following Bridget's confession of love. Lady J convinced herself she was happy in a FWB scenario, but ultimately, we will always want more.

Random Acts of Disappearance

They will give you just enough to keep you hanging, putting in appearances here and there but not enough to create a sense of an actual relationship between you. If you ask him to meet your friends and family, he may disappear for weeks on end in a puff of smoke. He may be on the phone to you every day one week then disappear for weeks at a time. Random Acts of Disappearance or R.A.D.s are common themes in E.U.M. relationships. Too much closeness all at once is just too much and so R.A.D.s are essential for breathing space. Sometimes Batman is so exhausted from wearing his costume that he needs a good old cup of cocoa and feet up in his comfortable home that you probably haven't been to!

Boomerang Boy Behaviour

Boomerang Boys are boys who drift in and out of your life with no announcement or even goodbye. They charm you with hearts and flowers then disappear out of your life with no warning; however, as soon as you start to get on with your life, just like magic he's back! Boomerang Boy will offer heartfelt apologies, promising you that he's changed. He may even tell you he has no hidden agenda and will become your best friend and confidante. You tell him all the ins and outs of your life with your boyfriend, and he listens compassionately, telling you how much you deserve better (forgetting, of course, that he ran off with your best friend and had a whirlwind secret affair). Of course, Boomerang Boy is there to offer a shoulder to cry on when it all falls to pieces, and hey! Presto! He's wormed his way back into your life! Don't get me wrong—there are Boomerang Boys who can be Soul mates. The ones you just can't live without no matter what happens; the Universe will always pull you back together. I am not talking about these types of Boomerang Boys. I am talking about the ones who like to come and go. The ones who like to enter your life in a helicopter and leave through the back door. These are usually Emotionally Unavailable Men who cannot and will not go the distance with you, yet they don't want to let you go completely. The attachment he feels is comfortable and suits his needs as he does not ever have to fully commit.

It is important to note that being Emotionally Unavailable is not gender specific. Emotionally Unavailable simply means not being emotionally or physically present to provide the love, trust, security, and stability a relationship needs.

Why Do We Select These Men?

We may select these men because we are attracted to the sense of mystery surrounding them or the charm they exude. These men can conceal their true identity. They believe they can be anything they want to be to you. They often exude such charm we want to hop on the ride and see where it takes us. However, five months or even five years down the line, the reality is we have been left high and dry in a game of merry-go-round with little but a sense of low self-esteem and a load of baggage he left us.

We may choose this type of man because perhaps we are attracted to his bad-boy image, believing we can pin him down and be the one to 'change' him. He becomes the latest project. How many of us want to be the girl to change James Bond or tame Batman? We sometimes become so embroiled in the mystery and sense of 'wildness' he projects we become obsessed with ripping off his costume and revealing the true Self. The question we need to ask ourselves is: would we be so enamoured with the "boy-next-door"? I think if we discovered Batman was just plain Billy from the block, we would be hugely disappointed. What we must remember when dealing with the E.U.M. is that oftentimes what we really discover is just an insecure man whose feelings of inadequacy and fear of commitment have led him to creating a false persona that can be maintained for only a very short period of time.

Some women are attracted to E.U.M.s because they pity them or want to save them in some way. Again, why attempt to fix that which is broken to the detriment of breaking yourself? When we try to fix those we are in a relationship with, it always comes with conditions. The real reason we want to fix a man is so that he can become the person we want him to be for us. When we try to fix with these conditions, we will always be the ones who will be broken. We form a co-dependent relationship where we live a life without boundaries and cater so heavily to the E.U.M.'s needs we totally abandon our own!

A good exercise to try is to divide a blank A4 piece of paper in two; on one side write a list of your needs, and on the other write what he is actually providing in relation to that need. That way you can have a crystal clear reality check that measures and identifies Your needs in relation to what you are actually getting. Sometimes it is easy to believe that because a need may have been met once or twice, then everything is alright. So it is also important to assess how regularly that need is being met. For example, it may be important to spend time together with your partner. If that need lacks consistency, then is that really enough for you? It is important to be honest about our needs and not to forget their value.

Finally, we may attract these men because perhaps we ourselves are Emotionally Unavailable. We attract into our experience what we reflect. Our stories of emotional baggage and unresolved attachment issues may resonate so deeply with each other that you become two magnets bashing ferociously together and abruptly swinging apart in a two-way game of hide-and-seek. There may be an attachment of some sort; however, neither party is emotionally or physically available to provide the other with the stability and commitment that a meaningful relationship needs.

Write a Letter to Your E.U.M. Letting Him Go

Dear _____

_____

_____

_____

_____

_____

_____

_____

_____

_____

_____

_____

_____

_____

_____

_____

_____

_____

_____

_____

_____

_____

_____

Chapter 7: Mr Loose Eye

Guilt

One night I was out with my friends celebrating one of their birthdays, and we were on the dance floor of this bar and it was really, really packed. Everyone was stepping on one another, and it was so hot in there that I remember complaining about it. We danced anyway. At one point this group of guys walked behind me to get to the other side of the dance floor, and I accidentally elbowed one of them in the junk while dancing. I had no idea this guy was standing there. I would never do it on purpose. I turned around to apologize, and with a smile on his face, this guy said, "You owe me a drink for that one!" I laughed and agreed, we got him a drink and chatted for a quick second, and he made his way back to his friends to call them over to my friends. We danced and chatted until the bar closed, and then we exchanged numbers.

After leaving the bar, I got a text message from him saying he wanted to meet up at a diner to continue to get to know one another. I had nothing to do, so I met up with him and we talked until the sun came up. He told me he was in the Air Force and that he was in town for a family funeral. We talked all about his experiences while deployed, and he shared funny stories about some of the folks he worked closely with in the Air Force. I still remember cracking up at his impressions of one of the ladies. I loved it. He also told me that he would be leaving to go back to Afghanistan the following day and that he would be gone for six months but that he wanted to keep in touch with me when he got back. I really liked this guy and I remember worrying about him when he texted the next day saying he was driving to the airport.

A week later I got a text message from him saying he was home again. I was so shocked and confused, but I couldn't wait to see him again. He said he had thought about me all week and had to see me. He picked me up later that night and we headed to a local diner for coffee. When we got settled in, he told me that the real reason he was in touch with me that night was because he wanted to tell me that ... he was married. He had no wedding ring on either time I saw him, and he never mentioned the wife that he lived with who is also in the Air Force. He actually admitted that he hadn't thought about her the entire time he was with me and that he was never being deployed that week—he just told me that so that he wouldn't have to figure out how to hide me from his wife. We eventually decided that we would be better off not being in touch, and I haven't heard from him since.

I share this story because I hear so many people, mostly women, say things like "my husband/boyfriend would NEVER cheat on me." We would all like to think this, but sometimes people don't set out with the mission to cheat. Sometimes you are just elbowed in the junk, and the next thing you know you're telling lies and feeling guilty that you're thinking about someone else all week. Now there's no need to be paranoid about this, but it's something to think about. Never say never. It happens sometimes, and I don't necessarily think that this guy's attachment to me was indicative of his lack of feelings for his wife. I think he simply enjoyed my company and I enjoyed his. I think the lies tore him apart faster than some people, so his wife is lucky that he can't stray too far without clearing his conscience, but everyone is different about these things. What if I had not decided to call things off with him? Who knows what could have happened.

Starlily, 28, Bristol, England

The Wedding's Off!

We met at an ice cream banquet. He was the cousin of my best friend, and honestly at first, I didn't even like him. After a perfect first date, though, we took off by storm. It was a wonderful relationship and one of my best days was when I agreed to marry him. Both our families got along. We both came from Christian backgrounds, and we were just perfect together (or at least so we were told). After about two years, he got a job out of town and would come into town for only one week every month, but this didn't stop us from having a wonderful relationship. We got engaged. It was a wonderful evening.

However, soon after, he began to ignore my text messages—and me as a person—but we still continued with our wedding planning. Then, on the day that the hall we wanted had made a reservation for us, he told me he wanted us to take some space. After a heated argument and amidst the chaos and upheaval, a female friend of his on Facebook, who I actually hadn't met before, sent me a request. I accepted and she started being overly friendly, saying how she is getting married and how she wanted me to attend her wedding. She would send me pictures of different wedding dresses and ask my opinion about which one she should choose. This girl would message me like 50 times a day. (I even wondered if she was gay!)

However, the day my fiancé and I finally broke up, all her messaging stopped instantly. I quickly connected the dots though I didn't have all the evidence. Although I had my suspicions, I didn't point any fingers. What made me point all my fingers is when she put up a message on his Facebook wall saying "Congratulations you're now a father. I will continue to make u a very happy man." MAN! Well, that's when I tripped. And when I say "tripped," I exploded so bad that family became involved! It wasn't pretty, but it would have been worse if I had married him. I just went on to thank God for a lucky escape and went on a vacation. I have never spoken to him since. I know I am better than that, and I am so much better off without him.

Tonisha, USA

Loving Myself First

To the women who think they just can't live without him— you can. To the women who don't think they are strong while they are alone—you are. But you love him, you say, and he loves you too? Well what about your love for you? After two years of paying 95 percent of the bills on my own and dealing with his infidelity, arguments, fights, and foolishness, I finally put my fiancé out. I can't tell you how many times that I told him I would, but after prayer last night, I did. He had not a dime of his own money, and I gave him $50 to leave with. He told his friends that he has no idea what happened—I just told him he has to go. That's OK.

It HURTS to let someone go when you love them SO MUCH that all you want is for them to be happy. But in the middle of me making him happy, I was sad, angry, resentful, and just plain UNHAPPY! I convinced myself that everything would be better once we married. I told myself that if I just gave him time, he would grow up and take on the role as man of the house and treat me with respect. No! What had to happen first was that I had to love myself more than I love him; I had to have more respect for myself than I have for him. I'm 30 years old now and I divorced in 2008. I have an eight-year-old son who has witnessed the utter disrespect that I ALLOWED! Now pregnant with my ex-fiancés child, I will be a single mother of two children.

I repeated my own history and my mother's as well. The only thing different is that I didn't go through with this marriage! I broke that cycle! I'm now looking forward to getting BACK on the path, with Jesus leading the way. I'm hurt, but I'm healing!

This is to those who may think it's too late, you're in too deep, you can't change the situation, or whatever the case maybe. Here is my story:

R.D. and I were childhood friends. His cousin and I are best friends (19 years)—so more like sisters. One day her brother came to visit me at my home. After greeting "my little brother," I see a short, light-toned gentleman dressed in an A-shirt underneath a button-down, striped, long-sleeve shirt and some khaki pants. To this day I remember his walk was smooth like butter. In my view he was walking in slow motion. "You know this is (R.D.) from when we were little, the one who was playing with me while you and Sis were playing Barbie dolls." Instantly I remembered the little boy who used to get on my nerves. He is still goofy like a child but talks like he knows how to handle business.

I called my "little sister" to get the scoop on him, and she said at the time he was not working, but he was looking and had some job interviews lined up. He's a good guy—young—but has a good head on his shoulders. Well, after texting, talking, dinner dates, and spending time with him and his cousins, our friendship advanced quickly to relationship (including him moving in with me). Anyway, about a couple months later, he started working with his cousin. R.D. and his cousin carpooled. I started noticing that sometimes he would stay gone with his cousin for days. I let him know if our living together was too much and he preferred to stay with his cousin, then he could do that. R.D. insisted on trying to get used to a live-in girlfriend.

Fast forward to March 2012 to The Phone Call. I fell asleep on the couch while watching television because I was sick. I woke up to hear whispering in my bedroom! I walked in and R.D put his phone down hurriedly. He was talking to someone he met on a CHATLINE! CHATLINE! So I started packing his stuff up and let him know I was not having this type of disrespect! He said they were just friends. I talked to her. She said they were just friends, but she didn't know he had a girlfriend. Well, I put him out for three days. And I was distraught! I couldn't cope with not being with him.

He came back with promises, saying he was so sorry and he should've known better, etc. Well, off and on between Facebook and Mocospace, there were repeat offenses. Along with being unfaithful, he had had three different jobs and was once again unemployed by the time September 2012 came along. I stuck with him. I had the mindset that he was young and would grow out of it. He would mature enough to provide for the family—after all, that's what he kept telling me. So October 2012 came and he eventually got a job, although it was part time. For the last year I'd been paying all the bills. I'd got my car fixed and was taking care of me, my son, and making sure his son was taken care of too.

We started to argue about bills and continued to argue about the other girls. He said he didn't know why he talked to other women—he was just scared of love.

Well, in between dealing with the 'women issues' and when I thought they had ceased, we got engaged. I bought a new car. (His name was not on it.) He was still working a part-time job and was only able to pay the gas/electric bill and put gas in the car. I paid the rent, car payment, car insurance, both cell phone bills, put groceries in the apartment, etc.

June 2013 I find out I'm pregnant. I let him know once again that he needs to make a decision on getting a 2nd job, a full time job, or leaving. I can no longer take care of everything. He promised to get a better job but barely went out to apply for jobs. Then a few weeks ago his coworker was here and says "R.D. is a player and hollers at all of the women." I shut down completely! He was still up to his tricks, not providing for our home, and I'm pregnant! I had to wake up and move on.

All night Friday night I prayed. I reminisced and sought out a solution that could benefit everyone. The only thing I received was that I stopped putting God putting God first a long time ago and in order to get back to order, a safe and stable home for my son, soon to be born and myself. Also R.D. has to grow up. He uses manipulation with the gift of gab to get what he wants, how he wants it, and when he wants it. I was blind because I didn't seek God first. Now he's blowing me up on Facebook about how much he loves me and we should work it out. I just keep looking at the holes in my walls and my door and think I was blind—not just to his lies but also to his abuse.

What's sad is I REALLY do miss him. I won't go back. I CAN'T go back. It's going on Day 2 and I'm getting stronger by the minute. The more hurt I feel, the harder I pray. I'm 15 weeks pregnant and everyone thinks I'm having a girl. I will find out next month, but if it's a girl, I have to show her that she is to put God first, value her body, know and show her self-worth, and demand respect as she respects herself. Funny! I didn't realize all the mistakes that I made until I wrote this out. Thank you! Even if you don't use this, THANK YOU ANYWAY! I needed to see my errors too! God Bless!

Gena, 30, Louisville, KY

Spot the Difference

Ring five differences between the two images.

Now list five reasons why you should lose your Mr Loose Eye.

1.

2.

3.

4.

5.

List five reasons why you are better off without him.

1.

2.

3.

4.

5.

List five things your experience with Mr Loose Eye has taught you.

1.

2

3.

4.

5.

Chapter 8: Parasites and Emotional Vampires Cause Abusive Relationships

Parasites are Emotional Vampires who feed off their partner in order to gain a sense of power and control. These types of people can be found not just in relationships, but in our everyday life. They can be family members, so-called friends, associates, and colleagues. However, forming intimate relationships with them and trying to form loving bonds with these sorts of people will almost always end in some sort of abuse. This type of abuse can be mental, emotional, or physical. They will drain you of your energy, your love, and sense of self-worth. Worst of all, they can make you doubt your own mind, decisions, and values. When a person is not mentally or emotionally stable themselves, unhealthy attachments are formed. Abusive relationships occur because the abusers themselves are often so damaged they are unable to love. Instead of loving, caring, and protecting their partner, they try to control, manipulate, and possess their partner, as if they are some sort of object to control. Abusive people themselves are victims of unresolved issues and unhealthy thought processes and can be driven by jealousy, resentment, hate, and fear. Abusive people are not happy people, but they often transfer their lack of self-worth and issues onto their partners so that they can hide behind a façade of false power and often charm.

Often we stay in these types of relationships because we feel we can somehow help this 'broken' person and try and show them how to love; most of the time, however, it is because we ourselves do not feel worthy of love. We often repeat the same abusive cycles that we have faced in childhood and so feel that these sorts of manipulative and unloving relationships—based on power, manipulation, and control—are in line with what we deserve. What we often fail to recognise is that it is not the abuser who has the control but us; it is not the abuser who doesn't love us how we deserve, it's us; and it's not the abuser who does not see our worth, it's us.

It is not the abuser that holds the power. We hold the power. We have the control because we have the freedom of choice to stay or to leave. We have the freedom of choice to love ourselves and find someone in alignment with what we deserve or stay in a relationship that beats us down mentally, emotionally, and physically. The following stories are written by strong and inspirational women who, in some cases, were victims of abuse from young ages as well in their relationships. They are testament to the fact that self-love is the key to finding the courage to exercise the greatest gift of all: the freedom and power to walk away. May all these women inspire you to remember who we are: strong, powerful, and loving human beings who deserve to be loved.

Lost

I met Kevin when I was just fourteen years old. He was fifteen going on sixteen and I met him through a friend whose boyfriend lived two doors down from him. We started dating almost straight away. He would sit on the wall where I lived and would meet me every day when I arrived home from school. At that age I had curfews which was hard because he didn't so you can imagine how often I was in trouble for being late home all the time! I really liked him. He was sixteen and a free spirit from home life.

Months went by when he told me he didn't live at home and that he in fact was in care waiting to be re-housed. His mum kicked his ass out the door as he was never at school and was in constantly in trouble with the police but that didn't bother me. I was too young and was head over heels in love with him. Had I'd been older I would have seen the sign but love got the better of me.

We moved in together when I was seventeen. I was working and he had odd jobs here and there. My family and friends kept on at me saying, "he is no good for you" and "he will come to nothing and only drag you down with him" but I didn't listen. After a year, he would drink more and more despite being unemployed. On a rare occasion, I would go out with friends to enjoy myself but he would say things like, "get that shit off your face you look like a slut!!" Sometimes he would bring down my confidence by remarking on my weight. He would say things such as, "I think you need to change you look fat!!" It became such an issue that I stopped going out. I fell pregnant and everyone around me was shocked but not happy for me. This made me feel I needed and wanted Kevin even more as he promised me the earth. I went on maternity leave and had my beautiful baby. I named her Keeley. She was my new world and he was a great 'hands on' dad. However, when I planned to return to work he started drinking again. We had little money and I had to turn to family to help. He would stay out all night drinking. When I told him that had enough, he promised to change.

On the morning of my first day back to work, he started to tell me that and started to tell me that I needed to sort out a babysitter as he refused to have her. I was rushing out the door with my six month old baby to get a train and I fell with her in my arms. I was devastated. Kevin called me a "stupid bitch" and blamed me for rushing. Thankfully I took the brunt of the fall and I vowed that day I will never put myself or my baby in that situation again. When I left my daughter with him while I worked, he would just lie in bed so eventually I gave up work to look after Keeley. We would often sit in silences for weeks at a time but after that he would be lovely again and everything seemed ok.

Soon after, I feel pregnant with Luke and Kevin just got worse. He would question my every move. I ended up hiding everything I bought for the children to save the rows. The name calling became so bad that I lost all the confidence I ever had. He also had an affair and had a baby with another woman. My confidence was at such a low that I still took him back. Then one night we had an argument over his drinking and he put a knife to my throat digging it in and telling me what I was and what he was going to do.

The police were called and he was arrested. When the police asked me if I was being abused I'd laugh and say "no way." However, things got worse and I started to realise that this could not carry on any longer.

I started to fight back. I just woke up one day and looked at my life and the life I had provided for my children. I took them with me and went to a homeless support organisation for help. They sent me to a temporary place where I would be safe but I didn't stay. I knew they would re-house me. I got an offer for a house and I thought I'm in now this was it! I thought if I can tell him I'm going I can do anything. I remember distinctly sitting on the end of the bed and telling him that I was moving out and that he could have the house and everything in it. I told him that I'd had enough. Then, bam he grabbed me. I just looked at him and said, "No. No more." I got off the bed, packed black sacks and left.

I moved into my house with nothing. A friend said there was a job going at a local school so I got a job there working a few hours a day. I also took students in and took a cleaning job and started driving lessons. I was able to take the children on little holidays. I also started to go out again and again and again. I was always out. My parents were great for having Keeley and Luke. Lots of men would talk to me but I never bothered. The more I was out, the more the weight came off and I became very confident. My sense of independence that had been taken from me for so long, returned and I think I became very arrogant as I had a lot of one night stands. In fact I had ten years on my own having a lot of fun. I seemed to meet a lot of men who were drinkers and one day I thought to myself, Anne you're just going round in circles with one drinker to another. I just couldn't settle with anyone. I wanted to keep men at a distance. I felt if I kept them at a distance then I was in control of them and not the other way round. But I found myself just attracting those who just loved drinking far too much until one day my friend said, "Anne I know the perfect man for you."

I was 32 and had lost all hope. I didn't believe her as I believed that men were all the same controlling pissheads. Then I met him. Rob from Bermondsey. He was living with his sister in Plumstead. He'd magically turn up at places I was out enjoying myself each week. He paid me lots of attention so I'd lap up the fact that he would buy me drinks and dance with me but then I would lose my confidence and start to think that getting close to him was wrong as he was not for me as he was too nice. I would tell my friend that something was not right. However what wasn't right was that I felt I didn't deserve him. After a few months of just seeing him in the pub, he looked at me and said, "We will be married." I laughed at him and from that day I was horrid to him.

Every time I saw him, I'd talk down to him. My friends would say, "Anne, don't be so nasty to him. He is a lovely man." I would simply reply, "No. He told me we would be married. He's a control freak just like all men." Then one night he asked to take me out and I found myself starting to like him but every now and then I'd be horrible to him. I wanted to be in control not him. I will see you when I want not you kind of thing. We would do a lot as a family and Keeley and Luke really liked him. I wasn't sure of him. I still didn't trust him and I didn't know why. Rob would often say, "I will knock that wall down even if it kills me. Why won't you let me in?" I never really understood what he meant until now. Rob was so loving all the time. He always wanted to talk about everything and anything. I often asked him what he saw in me and he would always say, "A lot of love."

We married the following year. He was right about us getting married. He is my best friend now, my soul mate, my everything. My children adore him and so do my family. I found myself asking him why he stayed and put up with all my issues and horrible behaviour. Rob stared at me and simply told me that he knew the wall would come down once I learnt to trust him and that I was a loving person who lost the trust in men because of the abuse I suffered in my awful 18 year relationship. We laugh now as I always tell him how lucky he is to have me. I have learnt that you can't see that horrible person who treated you so badly in everyone. I learnt that not all men are monsters out to seek control. It took a long time to rebuild my trust in men and love again. I took a long time for me to let my guard down and let someone else in. But in the end, it took years of a man showing me the love and respect I deserved as a woman a mother and a human being to finally love again.

Anne, 44, Charlton, England

Hook, Line, and Stinker

I had the worst kind of Mr Wrong when I was 15. He hurt me physically and sexually for months. I literally have no idea what I was thinking in staying with him. I have no explanation other than I think I thought it was normal. I swore I would never allow myself to be in a destructive relationship again but I did! Stupidity really. I understand women who are afraid to leave, women who don't think they have another choice, women who stay for various reasons or simply because they love their partners, but I didn't even really love either of these men.

The first man was Scott. He was 21 and I was only 15. Sometimes I think back and wonder why I didn't think he was creepy, going out with a 15-year-old, but I must have thought it was cool, I guess. I can only assume it was insecurities or some kind of mental hold as I became a crazy person! I think I had a mini breakdown. I started getting into fights in the street, drinking heavily, doing drugs, stealing: the whole shebang. I'm not that kind of person and can only assume it was an outlet for what was happening behind closed doors. It was when I was about 17 that one day it hit me like a ton of bricks what he had done and what I had allowed him to get away with. I had literally blocked out memories for months of my life. This has ruined relationships I had in my younger years for not being able to deal with it and never telling a soul.

In fact, the day I told someone I was on holiday with some friends, and this lad who was a friend of a friend had come with us. We all got hammered and I poured my heart out to him one night. I woke up several hours later with him touching me. My trust in men had gone. Years later, I went out with a guy called Paul who got very aggressive when drunk and would knock me about a bit. His housemate used to hear and intervene a lot before he could do any real damage. I thought these experiences made me stronger, but in reality they just made me aggressive in life and very extreme in my behaviour. It has taken many years and many failed relationships and friendships to figure this out. It has made me very sad to write this, and I don't think I've ever accepted responsibility for my behaviour before now. (It's quite therapeutic to be writing about all this!!)

Years later, I went out with this guy called Alasdair. He was so handsome and soooo charming! Also an absolute head case! In fact, I am convinced he is a sociopath and that's not an exaggeration.

Unfortunately he didn't really choose me because he liked me he chose me because he was skint and needed a girlfriend with a job! I didn't figure this out for a while though! His parents were well off and apparently gave him a private income whilst he was "looking for work." I use that term very loosely. I would be happy to pay for dinner while he was job hunting because he would 'get in next time when he was a bit more flush..' Yeah right!! I would find that money was gone from my purse and he had me absolutely convinced his flat mate's girlfriend was a thief! He invented stories about her and even asked me if I wanted him to ban her from the flat! Of course I didn't want this as I had no proof it was her and because his flat mate was a friend of mine and I didn't want him upset. It may seem obvious to you reading that yes it was Alasdair taking the money in the end but I had no idea that actual people stole from loved ones!

He would be texting other girls and meeting them while I was at work AND it even turned out he was dealing drugs at the pub I worked at, which everyone bloody knew except for me!! What a catch! In the end, I was sick of catching him out in silly little lies (this was before I knew about the stealing and the drugs!) and was getting ready to end it. He was meant to be leaving for Dubai in a few weeks, so I decided to let it peter out instead. He had other ideas, and one night decided to tell me I was never good enough for him—too fat, too ugly, and various other insults too. I laughed in his face and left.

A few days afterwards, I met some friends after work at my full-time job (pub was part-time) for a few drinks. When I arrived, he was there and wouldn't leave me alone! Bloody cheek of it! Anyway, eventually we arrived at the pub where I worked, and my friend behind the bar asked me what had happened between me and Alasdair, so I told her all he had said to me. I didn't realise that behind me was my manager and he heard everything I said. My manager was a very good friend and went ballistic. Unfortunately for Alasdair, he chose that moment to walk into the pub. My manager was not only defending my honour, he was also mad because this was the guy selling drugs in his pub. He punched Alasdair so hard he knocked him out cold. I do hate violence and was upset that this was partly down to me.

About a week later, I met Richard though, so I was very happy! Alisdair needed surgery as his cheek was broken. He told everyone I had asked my manager to do that and that he could no longer go to Dubai as he needed surgery on the day of his visa interview and they wouldn't reschedule. All lies of course. A year or so later I met a recent ex-girlfriend of his who he had told that he was in a car accident and that's why he needed surgery. (She said the scar wasn't visible and he started the conversation about the 'scar', not the other way around. Bizarre.) He also told her we had split up because I ran off with his best friend!! It turns out he had met Richard at a party a few months before we got together. Apparently this means they were best friends. I also didn't meet Richard till after we had split up. So many lies! I just don't understand people like that, but I fell for it hook, line, and sinker! Or should I say stinker!

Jessica, 29, Northampton, England

Letter of Reason

I was 19 at the time and was in love with my then boyfriend Peter. I was an adult now, or so I thought, and wanted leave home where I lived with my parents and move in with Peter. Dad, however, solemnly handed me a three-page, handwritten letter outlining his rationale for me not moving out of home. They were valid grounds, but I read them with an air of annoyance and tossed the note away. (I wish I had kept it.) I do remember some of the list, which included:

Needing the financial support of my parents to complete my degree

Living in an environment conducive to study

Looking after my health with my recent diagnosis of ulcerative colitis

That my Irish boyfriend (yet another Peter) was not the best choice of people to support me in the above ... and the list went on

They were all genuine concerns, coming from a place of love, and Dad could not have been more right; but as I mentioned, the letter ended up in the bin and I moved out.

I think that part of the reason for my belligerence was that I had reached an age where I didn't want to be accountable for every night out or every sleepover at a friend's house. What my parents didn't realise was that compared to many of my friends, I was a late bloomer and hadn't experimented nearly as much, or as early, with some of the things that went on at school. Also, coming from a household of three brothers, I felt there was a definite imbalance when it came to the freedom given to my brothers and the freedom given to me.

Dad was right though, and perhaps he saw through the happy-go-lucky character that Peter made himself out to be. Having been in the merchant navy in Ireland before he came to Australia, he was a big drinker, and it wasn't long before I discovered the many downsides of this. We enjoyed parties and pubs like most of our friends; however, it was about three months into our shared living arrangement that I was subjected to his alcohol-induced schizophrenia.

One evening on our walk home from a night at a pub called "The Geebung Polo Club", our happy banter suddenly turned to jealous accusations. I have always been the type of person to talk with someone if they speak to me. Isn't that manners? But due to my generally friendly and vivacious nature, several boyfriends have chosen to misconstrue this as flirting. I say "chosen" because it has always been a choice.

In an unexpected onslaught, I found myself slammed up against a parked car with allegations and fists flying. His posture was that of pure rage and his face red from the strain of his vehement and cutting bullets of abuse. He left me in the dark street and walked home on his own. With nowhere else to go at that time of night, my only choice was to dust myself off and drag my bruised body and bewildered mind back home. What the hell had just happened? Early that morning, he woke in a drunken daze, opened my closet door, and pissed on all my clothes.

Now most emotionally intelligent women would have packed their bags and left the next day ... surely. Conversely, after his profuse apologies and assurances that it would never happen again, I tucked the incident away and went on with life.

Everything was fine for a while. I had believed him when he told me it was a "one-off incident" and "totally out of character." When it happened again, I was just as surprised as the first time. This time we were at home, and some neighbourhood friends had popped in for pizza and a few drinks. As the night progressed, he became more obnoxious by the minute. I can't even remember what set him off, but I can clearly recall him shoving me up against the wall and holding the carving knife to my throat. My dog Pepe, although small, was as loyal and ferocious as any trained attack canine could be. He flew at Peter (well, at his ankles) in an attempt to save me from his wrath. The distraction worked, but Peter kicked my dog so hard in the ribs that he bounced off the opposite wall. Pepe just shook his head and went in for the second round.

It was about 3 a.m. and I knew I couldn't stay a moment longer. Peter went to have a cigarette, and I took this opportunity to make a call to my friends, Lynda and Shane. This couple had been my friends since high school, and they had always been generous of heart. Without a second thought, Shane jumped on his motorbike and made the half-hour trip to come and rescue me. With my helmet on and my dog bundled up between myself and Shane's back, we sped off to the familiarity of their safe and happy home.

Dad's dim predictions had become a reality. My studies had suffered along with my health. My University results were pathetic and my life in a shambles.

Jenny, 44, Sydney, Australia

Why I Never Drink Orange Squash

Joey is the father of my son. We met when I was just 19. What I thought was going to be a summer fling with a local bad boy became a nightmare I could never have imagined.

Tall, dark, and male-model gorgeous, I was completely, totally, deeply, head over heels in love with him. No man compared, and if he had asked me to lie down and die for him, I would have. He rapidly became the centre of my universe, and sacrificing family and friendships to be with him was easy. I felt blessed that I had found my Mr Right so early on in life and couldn't wait to spend an eternity with him. We shared our worries and our dreams. We laughed, we partied, we spent hour upon hour in bed. When I was with him, I felt invincible, as if we were the only two people on the planet who had ever felt this way, ever connected in this way. I loved how I would get home from work to hear the phone already ringing.

'Are you coming over?' he'd ask.

'Sure, what time do you want me?'

'Five minutes ago.'

Yes, I was young and stupid, and with the benefit of hindsight, I can see our infatuation with each other was not healthy. Neither of us was emotionally stable, especially after I lost our first child to an ectopic pregnancy. As supportive as he was during that time, our relationship became fraught. We'd moved into a tiny bedsit together but he was hardly home. I often sat alone, grieving our lost child. I remember one night he'd had enough of my tears. He got angry and started screaming and shouting and dragging me around the room by my hair—over furniture, into walls. My shoulder hit the window pane and it cracked. I knew I was going to have to pay for that at some point—financially and no doubt physically. I managed to crawl to the front door once he'd calmed down and left me in a battered heap in the middle of the floor, but his friend turned up and they pulled me back into the house, dumped me in the hallway, and locked the door. Joey's reputation when we first met had alluded to this aggressive side of him, but I'd never experienced it before and never thought for a second that his uncontrollable rages would be aimed at me. The next day I told him I was leaving him and that I'd arranged to stay with a friend a hundred miles away. He asked if he could come with me. I said yes.

I fell pregnant again almost instantly, and for a while, life looked pretty good. Our relationship went from strength to strength as we found a lovely apartment in our new town, got jobs, and prepared for the arrival of our baby. Five months into my pregnancy, Joey began using heroin. My Prince Charming changed almost overnight into the monster all children and adults alike fear.

He stole from me. He lied to me. He cheated on me. He beat me. He put me through every kind of emotional and physical torture a man can put a woman through. I feared for my life, his life, and that of our unborn child.

I'm not going to go into detail. I can't. Even now, fourteen years on, I have to stop myself from thinking of the horrible and degrading experiences he put me through because they are still too much for my head to cope with. Having been raised by an alcoholic father, you'd have thought I'd have been attuned to the nature of addiction. You'd have thought I'd realise that Joey's behaviour was a way to justify his drug use, a way to blame me when all the fault lay with him, a way for him to externalise his problems and not deal with them. Instead, I blamed myself for everything. Why was I not good enough? What did I do to deserve this treatment? Why wouldn't he just quit heroin and be a happy, normal family with me and our child?

Joey would disappear for days, sometimes weeks, at a time. I was sure he was running around with his drug-user friends. I knew he'd be out stealing and fighting. I knew he would be cheating on me. Yet I still sat there, night after night, praying that he was OK … praying that he wasn't dead in a ditch somewhere or had been arrested again. I'd jump every time the phone rang or there was a knock at the door. I was barely functioning with such high levels of stress and anxiety, and I quickly sunk into depression. My health was also deteriorating because of the lack of food in the house, and I knew I wasn't taking good enough care of myself during the pregnancy—not that I had a choice. He'd usually take all my money, and I became used to my limited diet of toast and orange squash. Weak, cheap, orange squash.

When Joey did return home, I was always apprehensive, worried about saying or doing something that would make him leave again. This, combined with the fear of his violent tendencies, meant I tolerated things I should never have had to experience. One evening he›d turned up with a friend. They began smoking crack and heroin in my living room while I was banished to the bedroom. He wouldn't let me out, not even to use the bathroom. I was eight months pregnant and had to urinate in a mug.

Yet I still loved him. I still wanted to make him better and give him the happy, loving family unit he claimed he'd never had. I found myself giving our relationship deadlines. I was sure that when the baby arrived, things would be different. I was sure that after our baby's first Christmas, things would be different. I was sure after this recent arrest and spell in a remand centre, things would be different. They weren't.

I beat myself up constantly for being a failure. For not being good enough. His words echoed around my head daily, 'You're a fat, lazy leech. You're useless. Nobody wants a single mother.' I believed him. When I walked in the street, I kept my head bowed, convinced that my ugliness would offend everyone if I looked up.

Overcoming the physical scars was easy. I quickly learnt how to disguise bruises and that broken bones would heal. It was the emotional torment that left a permanent mark on my mental health and altered my personality forever. My relationship with Joey is the reason I do not trust men. Or myself. It is the reason I jump to the worst possible conclusions all the time. It is the reason I have a barrier up against the world. It is the reason I cannot, no matter how desperately I may want to, make a relationship work with anyone else. My paranoia, self-loathing, and insecurities stem from the man who told me he loved me and then destroyed me. He never hung around to see the damage he had caused. He never tried to pick up the pieces. He never even said sorry.

Joey ended up in prison, and I used that opportunity to take my son and make a new life for us elsewhere. My son knows who his father is, and I make a point of never badmouthing him, but he is no longer involved in our lives.

It took years for me to realise I wasn't to blame for the situation I'd found myself in. I was the victim, the human punching bag for a man with deep, emotional issues that I could have never resolved. I also learnt that there are some questions in life you never get the answers to and that there is no point in over-analysing the whats, wheres, and whys of life. Some things just happen, and it's what you take from them that matters.

When my son started school, I went back to university. I graduated with an honours degree in theology and religious studies and went on to teach at secondary school. I am now a professional writer and home educate my teenage son. We laugh together all the time. He always tells me I'm beautiful and clever. I never drink orange squash.

Alison Klippenstein, 35, Berkshire, England

Don't Lose Yourself

It is so easy to lose ourselves in these abusive relationships. It is so easy to forget who we really are and become embroiled in the abuse and what somebody repeatedly tells us we are. It is hard to remember whilst we are in the situation what we deserve and how we deserve to be treated. It is also hard to remember that it is our responsibility, not anyone else's, to love ourselves unconditionally and look within for the validation and love we are worthy of. If you are or know anyone who is suffering in an abusive relationship, know that there is help available and encourage them to seek that help. Please see helplines on p. 171 We should not and do not need to suffer alone. Don't let abuse rewrite who you are.

Rewritten Soul

I opened up my Soul to you
Left it exposed to the naked eye
You opened the door, curious
And inspected the contents of I
At first you circled it, delicately
Treading ever so softly
Skirted around my **True** content
And inspected the content of I
Like a moth to a flame, my Brightness enticed you
Attracted to such light
Yet unwilling to See its origins
Or why I shone so bright
Eyes closed for so many years
Shut tight to Who I really Be
Too complex and three-dimensional
So blind you could not See
Threatened, you searched for a light switch
To drain away the "excess" energy
A switch, a plug, a wire
To erase it from my memory
Not content, somehow you penetrated me
At night you climbed into my skin
and sat upon
my Soul
Left your marks and scars and pains
Upon my bloody wrists
Tied tight were chains

Lost, forgotten and troubled Spirit
Origins covered with layer upon layer of fat
From his arse
I use to grab with delight
Swept under the carpet
Slicked back tight
Like nappy hair with a strong scent of unnatural chemicals
HER STORY no longer bears relevance
Masked, taped and filed away
Into the 'miscellaneous' cabinet

-Daniella Blechner

Websites and Phone Numbers

UK

This is Abuse - This is an excellent website for young people, both boys and girls, who want to learn more about abuse and what it is. It features a collection of video stories, myths, and a forum to raise questions. It has an extensive helpline directory for those seeking help all over the UK.

http://thisisabuse.direct.gov.uk

ChildLine

ChildLine is the UK's free, confidential helpline dedicated to children and young people

www.childline.org.uk

Heart

Heart is an EU-funded programme that offers help and advice to young people on having healthy relationships with boy or girl friends. It is particularly concerned where young people are feeling pressurised into something they don't want to do. It runs a 24-hour, anonymous, and confidential helpline, supplied by Childline.

www.heartprogramme.org

The Havens

The havens are specialist centres in London for people who have been raped or sexually assaulted. The havens help everyone—men and women, young people, and children of all ages. They can help you deal with and recover from the emotional and physical effects following an assault.

The havens are based in Camberwell, Paddington, and Whitechapel. To make an appointment, phone:

- Camberwell: 020 3299 1599

- Paddington: 020 3312 1101

- Whitechapel: 020 7247 4787

www.thehavens.co.uk

Samaritans

Samaritans provides confidential, non-judgmental emotional support for people experiencing feelings of distress or despair (including suicidal thoughts) 24 hours a day. They are there for you if you're worried about something, feel upset or confused, or just want to talk to someone. You can contact The Samaritans by telephone, email, or letter, or talk to someone in person in most of their branches.

www.samaritans.org/

08457 90 90 90

Women's Aid

women's aid
until women & children are safe
www.womensaid.org.uk

Women's Aid is the key national domestic violence charity that coordinates and supports an England-wide network of over 340 local domestic and sexual violence organisations running over 900 refuge, advocacy, and outreach services. Women's Aid campaigns for effective legal protection and services and works to prevent abuse through public awareness, education, and training. It also provides vital 24-hour lifeline services through the 24-Hour National Domestic Violence Helpline (in partnership with Refuge) and a survivors' message board on their website.

www.womensaid.org.uk

0808 2000 247

Respect

Respect runs support services and programmes for men and women who inflict violence in relationships. They also provide an advice line for men who are victims of domestic violence.

www.respectphoneline.org.uk

info@respectphoneline.org.uk

0808 802 4040

USA

National Domestic Violence Hotline They provide confidential, one-on-one support to each caller and chatter, offering crisis intervention, options for next steps, and direct connection to sources for immediate safety. Bilingual advocates are on hand to speak with callers, and their Language Line offers translations in 170 different languages. Their number is toll-free.

http://www.thehotline.org

1-800-799-7233 or 1-800-787-3224

T.E.A.R.

TEAR stands for **T**eens **E**xperiencing **A**busive **R**elationships. TEAR is an organization founded by teens in 2003 whose mission is to prevent dating abuse through education. We work to educate society about the complexities and seriousness of violent dating relationships.

www.teensagainstabuse.org

1-866-331-9474

US AND CANADA

To provide crisis intervention and support services to victims of intimate partner violence (IPV) and their families in order to help survivors recover from the trauma of IPV. We work toward the elimination of IPV by increasing public awareness and decreasing tolerance of IPV through community collaboration and education. DAHMW strives to improve the quality and safety of the lives of victims who are seeking peace in their homes and in their daily existence.

www.dahmw.org

Call 1-888-7HELPLINE

AUSTRALIA

1800RESPECT Call this number to access counselling delivered by qualified, experienced professionals 24 hours a day, seven days a week. If you are feeling unsafe right NOW, call 000.

NATIONAL SEXUAL ASSAULT, DOMESTIC FAMILY VIOLENCE COUNSELLING SERVICE

www.1800respect.org.au

1800 737 732.

WORLDWIDE

Hot Peach Pages offers a global list of abuse hotlines, shelters, refuges, crisis centres, and women's organizations, plus domestic violence information in over 100 languages.

www.hotpeachpages.net

Mr Wrong, Daniella Blechner

Part II

Journeying Within

Chapter 9: Why Do We Attract These Men and Relationships?

Start with You

These are self-esteem battering and, at worst, abusive relationships, and unless you want to keep experiencing the same death march each time, I strongly advise you take a deep breath, embrace a new approach, and follow these steps to Mr Right. But first it starts with you and the way you perceive yourself—how you feel about yourself. If you are ready to be honest with yourself and do some soul searching (it doesn't have to be a long and arduous task) and embrace a new approach, you are halfway there!

I have asked myself time and time again, 'Why have I deserved this treatment again?' I've even wondered why the world was punishing me. Why were most of my friends settled down and living happy, healthy relationships and lives and here I was, trawling through painful relationship after painful relationship, getting it wrong time and time again. What was wrong with me? Why couldn't they see what a catch I was? I'm intelligent, loving, caring, independent, vivacious, and positive. It took me over a decade to dissect the questions I was asking only to realise that I was asking the wrong questions. The question was not, "What is wrong with me?" but "Why am I attracting the wrong man for me?" The question was not, "Why can't they see what a catch I am?" but "Why couldn't I see what a good catch I was?" What was wrong with me was that I had allowed my sense of self-worth and self-esteem to be dictated and defined by the way these men had treated me. I had somehow subconsciously agreed that I had deserved it and, in doing so, kept on attracting the same type of man in my experience.

Now I imagine you're reading this now, protesting, "No I have a high sense of self-esteem and self-worth!" I did. Well, if that is the case, why do we keep attracting and staying with the same kind of unavailable men who hold us in such unsatisfying and negative situations? The answer is—it is us. It is **we** who are holding ourselves in this unhappy and unhealthy situation, **we** who have chosen this path, and **we** who have chosen this man. What we need to ask ourselves is, "Why have we chosen this particular man and path?" and "What are our expectations?" Deep down, do we expect these men to walk away from us, to hurt us and abandon us, or do we expect this man to offer us an equal, loving, and stable relationship based on honesty and mutual respect? If we expect the latter and get the opposite and still stay with him, what does this say about our sense of self-worth, our sense of self-esteem? Equally if we are expecting the worst and receive the worst and stay put, the same question can be posed: what does this say about our sense of self-worth, our sense of self-esteem?

Almost every woman on the planet has experienced a Mr Wrong at some point or other; however, if you are continually attracting these emotionally unavailable men, men who use and abuse us, perhaps we need to question if we are emotionally unavailable too? It would be utter madness to continue to point the finger without looking deeply within. When we are creating and recreating patterns in our lives, there is a huge lesson to be learnt. When we fail to take this opportunity to look within, we continue to stay on the merry-go-round and continue to tell all and sundry how awful our lives are. As Einstein said, "Insanity is doing the same thing over and over again and expecting different results."

Belief Systems

Belief systems are deeply ingrained beliefs we have about ourselves and the world around us. These are created and formed at an early age and affected by experiences and events we experience. Our belief systems can be affected by the way we are treated by others or made to feel. They can also be affected by other peoples' opinions or perceptions. For example, if as a child, you are told by people in "authority" or "authoritative positions" over and over again that you are clumsy, thick, and will never get anywhere, it is most likely that you as a child will not only hear these words, you will 'feel' these words and associate these words with yourself. Every time a child hears these words, they begin to believe these words apply to them. They will live out these words and most likely fulfil these false prophecies formed by someone else's misguided opinion. Belief systems create patterns in our lives and draw in whatever we believe to be true.

If someone is told they are "unlovable" as a child and they experience a lack of love from those who are meant to love them, most likely they will find it harder to accept and believe they deserve to be loved just for being who they are. Perhaps they will try and change who they really are in order to fit in or conform; hence, deep in their deep belief system they believe that in order to be loved they must conform; they must not be themselves. How long can a person live this way, concealing who they really are? How can a person really truly love themselves if they cannot be themselves? It is not healthy to live your life believing that to be loved you need to live by someone else's standards. Everyone deserves to be loved. No one is any more or less worthy. However, when we live through these kinds of experiences without being fully aware of the affects upon our own thinking or sense of self, we become littered with false and dangerous belief systems that have been dictated to us by those who, quite often, already have negative belief systems about themselves.

Childhood Experiences

Often, if we have lived through traumatic experiences, especially as a child, it will have an effect on the relationships you have with others. Similarly, if you have had positive experiences, these too will be reflected in the relationships you share with others. This is true of phobias and fears.

Take this as an example: I once visited a Healer who told me that I was attracting the same type of commitment-phobic man because somewhere deep in the blueprint of my thinking and belief system I believed I didn't truly deserve to be loved and believed that eventually, at some point, I would be let down. In addition, she also said that no matter how much I talked of having a family and settling down, I myself was a Commitmentphobe. As a result, I subconsciously attracted men I knew deep down would not be able to offer me the stability, security, and commitment a healthy relationship could offer me. As a result—wheel on Mr Commitmentphobe! Now I protested and protested until I was blue in the face, but eventually after seven years of protesting, I had to face some home truths. I realised that I had a deep fear of abandonment that stemmed from a deep sense of rejection and abandonment I felt as a child. This deep-rooted fear led me to attracting men either with similar childhood experiences or attracting men who would cause me to repeat the negative experience of abandonment and rejection again and again.

This deeply ingrained fear meant that I acted rather aloof in relationships. I never really made it clear whether or not I was bothered about the relationship or not for fear of rejection. Some men took this as a challenge, others as nonchalance, and others as rejection. I went through a stage where I actively feared attachment as it threatened my fierce sense of independence and inability to make decisions about what I wanted and needed. I wanted everything, yet I wanted nothing at the same time. Looking back, it was clear to see that I was a Commitmentphobe with a capital 'C', yet surprisingly I wanted to have a relationship that bought love and security at the same time.

I would push away men who wanted to offer me security and happiness and often attract men with the same fears and problems as myself, if not worse. I would not be attracted to men who were happy and "whole" because, unknowingly, I myself was not whole. Feeling comfortable and drawn to that vulnerability in them that resonated so deeply in me, I time and time again found myself falling into the role of the "healer", trying to fix and complete this part of him. What I hadn't realised is that these partners were acting as my mirror. Instead of fixing my belief systems, I abandoned them to spend my time "fixing" theirs.

I was eventually in a long-term relationship with a man who loved me intensely but suffered from anger issues due to his own experiences of abandonment. This relationship was the typical rollercoaster of highs and lows. When it was good, it was really, really good, and when it was bad it was horrid. I was an outgoing, vivacious young girl who enjoyed going out but turned in on herself because of his intense jealousy and accusations. I had always been fiercely loyal, yet I began to change the way I was in order to keep the peace. I began to tread on eggshells and watch what I said in case it would upset him. I lost myself and part of my identity as I was swept away with the whirlwind nature of the relationship. In saying this, we had a real connection; we both had a goofy sense of humour and enjoyed the same things. On the surface our relationship was loving, affectionate, and happy; however, it was also often traumatic, intense, and unhappy.

I eventually learnt to set boundaries and make strong decisions about what I would and wouldn't tolerate, and when that boundary was crossed, I ended it. It was the hardest thing I'd ever done, but I knew in my heart it was right. I wanted to date a man who could be a role model to my future children and that meant them seeing their mother being treated respectfully. That really was what it came down to for me. It took the idea of children who hadn't even been born yet for me to stand in my power and put myself first! Thank you, my future children!

I learnt that these types of relationships are often long-lasting as neither party can bear to abandon or separate from the other. This can be partly because they cannot bear to inflict that same type of abandonment they fear so deeply on the other and partly because they fear being alone. Worse still, in these types of intense and dependant relationships, you may end up catering so heavily to his needs that you abandon and reject your own. These are often emotionally abusive relationships, leading you right back to your own fears and insecurities held in your belief system: that you are unworthy of love; that your needs, wants, and desires are not important; that at some point they will be rejected anyway. However, if you have not placed your needs, wants, and desires high up on that ladder of importance, why would or should anyone else? The relationship I had attracted and the man I had chosen perfectly matched my deep-rooted belief that I didn't deserve to be loved (wholly and healthily) and that I will eventually be bitterly let down. Well, at least it was a perfect match! How could I possibly be a victim when I have simply attracted what I believed to be true?

Fear of Abandonment

Fear of abandonment is a genuine condition often rooted in childhood or traumatic experiences. You may have experienced abandonment, neglect, or rejection as a child or perhaps exclusion amongst your peers at school. You may continually question why you deserved to be abandoned or what was wrong with you. Because of your experience and lack of clarity on the situation, you may hold in your belief system a belief that you don't deserve to be loved and that everyone you ever love or become close to will eventually realise this and leave you. Sometimes this may cause us to act aloof or emotionally distant in a relationship; however, it can also have the opposite effect. You may be overeager to please, to be loved, to be validated. Any sign of rejection sends you falling down into an abyss of deep, dark fears that you will never be loved, are unworthy of love, and that whatever you have to give will never be enough. You tell him over and over that you're scared he'll leave you, that you don't feel good enough. You begin to constantly crave reassurance from your man and do anything you can to please him, only to find that after a while he's done the very thing that you feared—abandoned you. Your fears and insecurities took over and you've stifled him. You attracted the experience you paid most attention to—being rejected and abandoned. Until, as a woman, you feel good about yourself, you will always attract the same experience that brings you closer and closer to your fear. If you feel unworthy, why would any man feel that you are (worthy)? Think positive.

Mary Seacoles and Florence Nightingales

Mary Seacoles and Florence Nightingales are women who desperately want to "fix" or "heal" their man. They want to be that compassionate "Lady with the Lamp" who tends to and nurses hardened but broken soldiers and prisoners of war. Mary Seacole was a hugely determined lady who combated racism and funded her own journey to nurse soldiers who were victims of the Crimean war, often tending to them on the battlefield against all odds. Mary Seacole is a personal heroine of mine. However, too often we want to fix what cannot be fixed and heal what cannot be healed, at least not by us.

As women, we are natural "healers" and "fixers." I know I have an overwhelming passion to nurture and protect, to put right where things are wrong. As a child, I had a great sense of justice and putting right what was 'wrong.' I'd be the child befriending the newbie all alone in the playground, the child picking up hobbling woodlice and pigeons with broken wings in an attempt to fix and put right. I think I even set up a club could "The Help Club" of which I recruited one person who left because they realised that they did not get anything out of it! I learned the hard lesson that things couldn't always be put right, that living things must find their own way, their own journey to completion or happiness. And then, are we ever really complete? I remember finding a pigeon in the garden, its wing broken and bleeding after a cat had got to it. I put it into a box and carried it all the way down to the vet, filled with glee that they would fix the pigeon and it would one day fly again, only to go back to the vet the next day to be told nonchalantly that they'd had to snap its neck. Cruel to be kind, they said. I couldn't understand why we could cure chronic illnesses, fix broken legs and arms in humans, and recover from heart attacks but couldn't fix a pigeon's wing. It baffled me.

I experienced a strong figure in my life suffer awful bouts of stress and I couldn't understand what was wrong. Was I the cause of their pain and stress? I couldn't understand why I couldn't fix them. As an adult, I now understand it was part of their journey, their experience, personal to them. It wasn't for me to "fix" or to "force my judgement upon." Although I make light of 'Mr Wrong' and 'Mr Right,' inherently there actually is no such thing as "right" and "wrong", just journeys of lessons that add strings to your bows, wisdom to your knowledge, and, at times, countless grey hairs!! People and things that feel wrong at the time often put you onto the path of something that is so right for you. Take this book for example; if I hadn't had so many traumatic experiences with men who were wrong for me, I wouldn't be able to share these valuable stories, experiences and lessons from women and men all over the word. Nothing in our lives is wasted time. Experiencing adversity and setbacks does not make us bad or unworthy people, nor does it mean that there is something wrong with us. We can't always fix what **we** think is broken nor should we try to; we can only heal what exists within ourselves. But that wasn't in the handbook at 11 years old—or now for that matter!

We often feel a duty to help, and this can stem from childhood experiences, of not being able to fix or intervene in a situation you felt powerless over. Sometimes we try too hard to help, thinking we are doing them a favour or helping them to change and grow, but being your man's "Mary Seacole or Florence

Nightingale" is not going to do you any favours. These types of relationships end in resentment. You try and try and try to fix and heal and help, only to have your help thrown back in your face with a tremendous thump! You feel as though all the time, energy, and love you put into trying to help have gone completely unappreciated. Furthermore, you are made to feel like little more than a meddler and busybody, as though you don't understand them or what they're going through. They haven't felt the warmth, compassion, and love that you put into offering that help. They didn't see the tears in your eyes as they threw your advice out the window, tore your heart out of your chest, and smashed it hard against the wall. There is a difference between guiding and lovingly supporting and forcing our help on another. Forcing your help on another can hinder others from learning and discovering their own lessons themselves. The dictating, preaching and desperate desire to help will only create resentment in them.

They are resentful that you have to see them vulnerable, that they cannot provide, cannot protect, cannot express their emotions the way you can. Resentful, even, that they need you. They feel emasculated by their Mary Seacole and stifled by things he cannot provide for himself. You make him confront his fears and issues, but he's not ready to see them. Life is a beautiful thing to witness. As a child, I loved watching caterpillars transform into their cocoons, emerging many days later into beautiful butterflies. You would never push a caterpillar out of a cocoon, would you? No. It needs to be self-sufficient, to utilise its own resources in order for it to grow. You can offer it unconditional love and support, but you would never push it out. It's the same with your man. Stop pushing and let him arrive at his own understanding.

Know What You Deserve

We are beautiful women who are trained to remain strong and loving in adversity, to stand by our man through thick and thin. But what if our man is not sticking by us? What if we deserve better? First, we must know better. Be crystal clear about your expectations from a man and a relationship. What is it you want, need, and desire? What and where are your boundaries? What will you put up with and what will you not? What's important for you? Until we ourselves know the answers to these questions, we will be keeping our path open for the wrong man as the net spreads across the ocean. Why leave yourself open to everything and everybody when we can be clear on our intentions and expectations? We don't want any sharks lurking at the bottom of the ocean, thank you!

We do not need to leave ourselves wide open and expose our vulnerabilities to Mr Wrong. Neither do we need validation or permission to be loved. We are already loved if we already love ourselves, and we certainly do not need permission. Be mindful of our negative beliefs, thinking, and patterns, and aim to change the course of direction they are taking us. We can change them by thinking positively about ourselves and surrendering and making peace with our past experiences. Put them to bed. They have no place in our present or our future.

Now, I'm not for a minute saying to stay away from men who have had traumatic experiences, nor am I saying that if we as women have experienced unpleasant relationships or had traumatic experiences we can never have a successful relationship. What I am saying loud and clear is do not let them dictate who you are and how you behave and, more importantly, how and what they make us feel or believe about ourselves. It is not just women who hold these belief systems within us; it's men too. Just as we want to feel good about ourselves and believe positive things about ourselves, we want to attract a man who truly feels good about himself too. An unhappy man cannot love a woman fairly or healthily until he himself is happy. He will only serve to make an unhappy woman unhappier and drive a positive woman into the depths of unhappiness. We must change our thinking and negative thought patterns to attract a positive man who is attracted to our positive thought processes.

Until we recognise, confront, and aim to change these negative thought patterns and belief systems in ourselves, we will always be attracting that which we most fear or think about. It begins with awareness. Awareness is the catalyst for change. Part of becoming aware is to accept and surrender to our fears. To be aware of them but do not feed them. Why feed an angry wolf when you can feed a loving one?

Give thought to that which makes us smile, laugh, and sing; to that which gives us a sense of hope and joy and belief in our dreams. Hold positive thoughts about the types of relationships we do want, not the ones we most fear. Mr Right not Mr Wrong.

I am saying that we need to recognise and acknowledge what we don't want before we can claim what we do, just as we must acknowledge our fears.

Native American Parable

An elderly Cherokee Native American was teaching his grandchildren about life. He said to them, "A fight is going on inside me. It is a terrible fight and it's between two wolves.

One wolf is evil—he is fear, anger, envy, sorrow, regret, greed, arrogance, self-pity, guilt, resentment, inferiority, lies, false pride, competition, superiority, and ego.

"The other is good—he is joy, peace, love, hope, sharing, serenity, humility, kindness, benevolence, friendship, empathy, generosity, truth, compassion, and faith.

"The same fight is going on inside you, and inside every other person too."

They thought about this for a minute, and then one child asked his grandfather, "Which wolf will win, Grandfather?"

The elder simply replied, "The one you feed."

Setting Your Intentions

I have, in the past, entered many relationships with no expectations at all. I've simply been drawn to someone and been happy to "go with the flow." Because I had no expectations or real intentions, I have found myself swept away with his ideals and his expectations and led down his path as to where the relationship should go and where the boundaries are placed. I cannot emphasise the importance of having balance in a relationship. Boundaries and expectations should be shared equally in a relationship. I found that my own "laid-back approach" quite often led to a jealous or intense partner who overcompensated for my lack of boundaries or a partner who simply lost interest as I failed to question where he was off to at night or allowed him to dictate how often we saw each other.

I am a fiercely loyal Sagittarian who believes in giving your partner space and freedom to experience the world in their own right in order to add more to the relationship. However, I realise perhaps this can be conceived by some as not caring, not being serious, or perhaps not even being bothered. Because of this free spirited energy and independence, men often feel that they do not have to make the effort. Sadly, we 'Ms Independents' we often end up with partners we know cannot give us what we need, yet we stay in the hope that things might change or that we may eventually be deemed 'worthy' of this person's time, energy, and love. What we fail to realise is that if this man is unable to give you the basic things that a relationship requires such as reliability, support, and love, then this man is unavailable no matter how independent we may think we are. We must remember that in order to have a healthy relationship, we too, as women, must be available. Like attracts like, remember. Read Sally's account of life with Mr Unavailable.

Wanting So Much More and Getting Nothing

I've been in relationships where all I've wanted to do was to spend quality time with my partner, go on dates, explore the world, spend the night together and wake up in the morning, spend time with each other's families, go to events together, and feel like a proper couple. Yet when I expressed these needs and intentions, I was made to feel like I was demanding. I was given countless excuses and false promises. The more I heard the excuses, the more frustrated I would feel. The more frustrated I felt, the more unworthy I would feel. The more unworthy I felt, the more desperate I would feel for a stable, loving relationship.

If I had understood and set my intentions and boundaries from the beginning and had higher expectations for myself, I wouldn't have hung on so long in an unhappy and unhealthy situation that made me feel so bad, one that battered my self-esteem and sense of self-worth. If I stopped defining myself by the way that I was treated and believed that I deserved better, I would have set off onto the path that led me to what I more closely deserved. If I had set my intentions and expectations from the start, I would have realised that this man was UNAVAILABLE.

Sally, 36, Toronto, Canada

Needs, Wants, and Desires

Needs, wants, and desires are very essential in relationships. Everybody has needs, wants, and desires that they would like to be fulfilled. The question is how often do we remember them? Have they ever been written down? In some cases we haven't even recognised or identified them until we are treated badly.

What Are the Differences between Needs, Wants, and Desires?

Needs are essential prerequisites we request to survive in a situation—the basics, as it were. Qualities or things we cannot do without. For example, we all have a basic need to be loved healthily, a basic need for respect. It is important to note that, whilst this list is of absolute importance, it is also equally imperative that we ask ourselves what we are doing to reflect the type of relationship we need, want and desire.

Wants are things we would like but will still survive without. For example, I want a car, but as I live in London and am close to an abundance of transport links, I do not NEED one desperately. However, wants in relationships are again essential as we are choosing and setting intentions regarding the kind of relationship and man we want.

Desires are add-ons, things we really, really want but again can live without. They are luxuries that we crave and deep down dream of and yearn for. For example, I desire to go to Cuba this summer, visit Brazil, and camp out in the Amazon; however, practicalities and real life mean I may not necessarily do those things. Desires are something to aim for and never give up on. Look at the example exercise below and try it for yourself. Don't worry if you become stuck or are not sure what you need, want, and desire. If anything, this exercise will get you thinking and setting your expectations and intentions. Go for it! You deserve to be fulfilled!

Exercise – Needs, Wants, and Desires

What Do I Need?

I need a man who respects me.

I need a man who is reliable.

I need a man who is kind and generous, loving and affectionate.

I need a relationship that is equal.

I need a relationship that is based on trust.

I need a relationship that is happy and healthy.

What Do I Want?

I want a man who will take me out on dates regularly.

I want a man who listens to me compassionately.

I want a man who supports and encourages me.

I want a relationship that has plenty of laughter.

I want a relationship that is full of passion.

I want a relationship where each other listens to the other.

What Do I Desire?

I desire a man who pampers me with massages and foot rubs once in a while.

I desire a man who takes me out on romantic dates.

I desire a man who enjoys travelling to exotic locations with me.

I desire a relationship that is full of romance, passion, and love.I desire a peaceful yet exciting romantic relationship that results in a long-term marriage.

I desire a relationship where we travel extensively and enjoy exploring all corners of the Earth.

Exercise – Needs, Wants, and Desires

What Do I Need?

I need a man who

_____

I need a man who

_____

I need a man who

_____

I need a relationship

_____

I need a relationship

_____

I need a relationship

_____

What Do I Want?

I want a man who

_____

I want a man who

_____

I want a man who

_____

I want a relationship

_____

I want a relationship

_____

I want a relationship

_____

What Do I Desire?

I desire a man who.

_____

I desire a man who

_____

I desire a man who

_____

I desire a relationship

_____

I desire a relationship

_____

I desire a relationship

_____

Setting Your Intentions

Now that you have established your needs, wants, and desires, let's begin on setting your intentions. An intention is a higher-consciousness thought. It is a desire expressed with absolute faith that the outcome will transpire. An intention is an expectation simply handed over to the Universe in order for it to be fulfilled—a bit like placing an order at a restaurant and then waiting for the meal to arrive. When we place the order or express the intention, we expect the meal to arrive. We don't hound and harass or follow the waiter into the kitchen to ensure they have placed the order correctly or get into the kitchen and start cooking it ourselves. We have faith that the order will arrive. Just as we say thank you when we place our order and again when our order arrives, we must do the same with our intentions. Gratitude plays a major role in intention setting.

To set an intention, first we must become aware of our thoughts. What do we think about most? How do we feel about love, relationships, and life in general? Do we think negatively or positively? Whilst we may think these thoughts do not play a role, they play a vital role in setting and living our intentions and dreams. What we focus on consciously or subconsciously will every time become our reality.

First look at your needs, wants, and desires in the exercise above and change the sentences so that they read: I have a man who respects me. I have a man who is reliable. The subconscious mind reads this as something you have already achieved and so will seek to attract that into your life. Writing in the "I am" or "I have" form is extremely powerful as the link is made between the subconscious mind and yourself. It means "Do it Now!" and kick-starts your subconscious mind into action to match your intention. "I want" or "I need" still works, but the subconscious mind reads this as something you don't already have and so will work slower to achieve it than if it is a direct intention such as "I am" or "I have." Many successful people will tell you that they achieve their goals through visualisation, through believing that they had already achieved success.

Visualise the type of man you want to be with. Create a clear picture in your head and focus upon it. Concentrate on what you are attracted to. Is it his smile, his eyes, his laugh? Now imagine the positive qualities you need, want, and desire in this man, and gradually build a picture. Do not allow any negative thoughts or doubt to enter your mind. If they do, just take note of them and send them along their way. They have NO place in this exercise. Don't limit yourself. Work it! You deserve all that you focus upon and visualise.

In your mind or aloud read out your intentions or affirmations in the "I have" form. Example: *"I have a man* who respects me." *"I have a* relationship that is equal." Reading these affirmations aloud or simply focusing upon them in your head will kick-start your subconscious into positive action and will almost immediately begin to bring these positive opportunities and chance meetings into your life. If you don't believe me, just try it. What is there to lose? If you want to keep attracting Mr Loose Eye, The Dreamer, or The Serial Liar, then keep on focussing on the pain and upset they caused you and why life is so unfair. If you want something better, try something new.

Vision Boards

Vision boards are a collection of images placed on a board. The images can be drawn or selected from magazines, papers, or adverts, but they must represent all things positive you wish to manifest into your life. For example, if you are looking for marriage, stick images of beautiful brides and grooms, wedding rings, and dresses on your board. If you want more money, stick images of pots of gold or notes. If you wish to own property abroad, flick through travel brochures or property brochures and select images of houses you wish to own in the future. Stick all these on your vision board and place it somewhere you will regularly see it, perhaps just before bed and before waking up. Use your affirmations and intentions and focus upon them while studying the images. For example, if you want to attract a man who owns a yacht, loves children, and can offer a woman all the love, security, respect, and honesty she deserves—oh, as well as a ring—then focus upon him and focus upon your intentions. If you want a man who loves and respects you, imagine what it **feels** like to be loved and respected. Focus on the feeling

It can also work for making changes from within. If you want to gain more money or heal from a past situation, set your intention: "I have an abundance of money" or "I am healed and happy." Again, imagine this scenario; focus on how it feels to be healed and happy or to live in abundance. Gratitude is extremely important, and so as we finish setting our intentions, we must have absolute faith that it will arrive and we must give thanks to the Universe or our subconscious brain for making it happen. Now, whether you believe in miracles or not is another book; however, one thing can be said with the utmost confidence: these positive affirmations train your brain to think differently about yourself and life itself. They train your brain to start thinking positively about love and relationships, to release negative belief systems, and to focus upon that which gives us joy and complete happiness. Try it today!

Chapter 10: The Gates of Heaven Swing Open

Sometimes when we start to let go and set our intentions and expectations higher, significant people seem to resurrect themselves from your past and pop up again. Have you ever experienced this? Just as you take those steps into a more positive future, that Old Ghost From Christmas Past is ready for a cameo role in your life.

So here's the scenario. You've been dating a man for a few months now. You're taking it slow. He, on the other hand, seems full on and wants to race full-steam ahead into a full-on relationship. You begin to let him in; you open your heart up to him. Then ... before you know it, he's closed the door and shut you out, leaving you engulfed in darkness with no explanation. You wonder for months what you did wrong, and you batter yourself with thoughts such as, Why me? What if I ...? Perhaps if I had ...?

These thoughts swim around and around in your mind as you point the finger within. As you point the finger within, your confidence fades, your self-esteem begins to wither, and your self-worth begins to decrease. Each time you rehash what you could have possibly have done wrong to deserve this treatment, your belief about what you think of your own sense of self-worth screams, "I deserved it!" "I am wrong!" "I am unworthy!" "I am not good enough!" Each time you play out scenarios in your mind and criticise every feeling you felt, every word you expressed, or every action you took, you tell yourself, "I am not good enough."

Well you **are** good enough. This man simply did not recognise your value or was not able to accept you in all your shining glory—The Good, The Bad, The Ugly. For that is truly what real love is; anything less is simply an illusion.

So as you beat yourself for not being:

- Understanding enough

- Patient enough

- Available enough

- Caring enough

- Pretty enough

- Intelligent enough

you slip into the role of a victim who allows people to treat you badly. Look at the list above. Cross out "enough" and write "I am" before the first word.

You are enough just as you are. The man who loves you the way that you deserve will tell you these words. Back to the scenario: you're moping around at home getting over a heartbreak. You may enter in and out of relationships, never quite feeling enough. Then, after a period of inadequacy and powerlessness, you gradually begin to get better. You get stronger. You rediscover Your Self again. You begin to heal. At that point, just as you begin to heal (now, this may be a few months or even a few years later) you receive a phone call, a text, or a Facebook message from Boomerang Boy from **Chapter 6** with a short message asking you how you are. He may tell you how sorry he is for how badly he treated you or that he'd like to take you out and catch up or even try again.

Now I don't want to batter Boomerang Boy for making contact and would certainly never reject an apology, but in my profession as a teacher, some may receive a serious late detention! "Better Late Than Never!" I've often had the temptation to scream. I've even had one beam down the phone at me after a year and a half of no contact, expecting me to recognise his voice without actually stating his name! For some reason I am the expert in experiencing Boomerang Boy and have had a total of six ex-boyfriends call me anywhere from seven months to two years after our breakup, apologising for the way that they treated me. Uncannily enough, four of them called whilst I was writing this book, including JudgeJustice from **Chapter 4!**

Sometimes these apologies are very humbling for both parties and can help create a sense of peace, understanding, and mutual respect. I have nothing but respect for anyone who offers an apology with sincerity and has the maturity to take responsibility for their actions, whether it be a week, month, year, or decade later. Accepting apologies also helps us take responsibility for our own actions and reactions. A relationship is a two-way thing, and sometimes we may be just as guilty as Boomerang Boy for the breakdown of a relationship.

On the other hand some of these men expect their "random reappearance" to be greeted with, "Oh my God! It's YOU! Where have you been all my life!?" The Boomerang Boys I am focussing on in this chapter are the ones who have hurt us and left us without the dignity of an explanation or acknowledgement of their undesirable treatment towards us. The ones with the ability to love like a king then vanish and reappear at a snap of their fingers with apologies, charmed words, and the expectation that all you have been doing for the past few years is sitting around waiting for him to reappear back into your life.

In October 2012, whilst writing this book, I had an ex-boyfriend ring me up completely out of the blue saying, "Hi, it's me!" When I was unable to distinguish who "me" was, he followed through with, "Can't you recognise my voice?" It's almost as if he expected the Gates of Heaven to swing open and cast down a blinding, white light to illuminate my pathway and guide me to the bright brilliance that was Him. "It is I. Come, Speak to me. You are now worthy in my Presence." It was as if he expected the angels to fly down and have me rejoice and praise his holy name (or holy voice in this case). Perhaps he wasn't so impressed with the half-hearted "oh" at the revelation of his name.

After meaningless waffle about what he was doing at the moment and memories of pet names we used to have for each other, he finally apologised for the way he treated me in the past before proceeding to talk about a "connection" he felt we had. Now this Mr Dreamer has swanned in and out of my life a total of three times, each time telling me how special I was and how he felt I was "The One," rushing ahead, talking about children and weddings. Each time we'd get close, and just as I started to let him in, he'd disappear with no prior fall out, argument, warning, rhyme or reason, and worst of all, no explanation. Two years ago I was desperate for an explanation for the hurt and abandonment he had caused me again—I would have got back with him in a heartbeat. However, this now being 2012 and the **third** time that he had done this, I felt well versed enough to accept his apology and politely tell him I was no longer comfortable talking with him.

It was hard for me to do purely because it went against the grain of my natural instinct. My natural instinct is to love, forgive, and be on good terms with everybody. However, I had to listen to my inner voice, and my inner voice was shouting "Enough!"

I realised then that I could still love, forgive, and part on good terms, but I didn't have to keep accepting other people's crap and have my emotions be defined by how others felt about me. I had to break the pattern and take the lesson that had been offered to me time and time again. I no longer needed his approval or validation. Validation and love must come from within.

My experience has made me stronger and wiser. Too often we hear from these Boomerang Boys months or years later, and because we have felt or have been 'made to feel' so low about ourselves, we validate ourselves through others' opinions or validations to mirror our own feelings of acceptance. The belief being: If I am accepted in such and such's eyes, then I am worthy enough.

Here's the process broken down on next page:

Boomerang Boy's Actions	How it makes us feel	What we now believe
Boomerang Boy shows us attention, affection, and love.	Loved, accepted. We approve of Boomerang Boy. We feel "right." Happy	He loves us. I am worthy. I am loved. I am validated. I am happy.
Boomerang Boy abruptly dumps us.	Abandoned Rejected Inadequate Unloved Unhappy We feel "wrong." Perhaps angry, betrayed	He disapproves of me. I am not worthy. I am not loved. I am not valid. I am unhappy. There is something wrong with me. Perhaps: I am owed an apology/I will never forgive him.
Boomerang Boy calls and repents.	Validated Appreciated Valued Needed Worthy We feel "right."	I am valid. I am worth appreciating. I am of value. He needs me. I am worthy. I am right. Perhaps: He can be forgiven. Justice is served.

The table shows that the person's feelings and beliefs about not only themselves but the situation are completely dependent on Boomerang Boy's actions. When this man is seemingly making us 'happy,' we feel validated, worthy, and somehow "right." "Right" as in we are right to feel good, we are right in our decision to be with this man, and all is right with the world! When Boomerang Boy has a change of heart, notice how quickly the feelings and beliefs change. Suddenly we feel unworthy, no longer valid, and unloved and rejected. These feelings greatly affect our beliefs, and our beliefs about ourselves swiftly plummet from feeling good to self-battering and self-depreciating. We may feel anger, hurt, and betrayal and believe we are owed an apology. This holding of anger and hurt serves only to hurt ourselves.

These feelings and beliefs again are completely dependent on Boomerang Boy's actions. If he does not apologise, how long do we expect to stay angry, waiting for an apology that may never come? Waiting for another to act or react in a way that we want them to only delays our own process of feeling good. Whilst we wait for an apology, we continue to feel unhappy and hard done by. It is also worth noting that some people go through these stages of validation, rejection, and back to validation again only to carry on the cycle again and again by accepting Boomerang Boy and his repetitive behaviour back into their lives. This cyclic dance can easily become one of power, control, and manipulation. In other words, it is a solid foundation for a toxic relationship.

Apologies from others should not be what validates us and makes us happy and worthy. We are.

What we need to remember is that we are beautiful by default, strong through adversity, and wise through experience. What we need to remember is that whilst apologies and forgiveness can be very humbling experiences indeed, we were worthy before, we **are** worthy whilst we are with him, and we **are** worthy now. Never let anyone dictate to you your worth. No human on the Earth has that power. Don't wait for Boomerang Boy to come back into your life; forgive him as part of your healing process. When or if he does ring you months or years later, accept his apology. Why? Accepting apologies means you are not harbouring any bitterness. Bitterness is the cause of illness and tension in your body. To accept and forgive another is to heal and cherish Your Self.

Now Boomerang Boy may have 'hidden' or not so hidden agendas to go back out with you or date you again. That is **your** decision and your decision alone to make. Do remember that people don't tend to change the way they treat you unless you change your beliefs or thoughts about yourself. Be clear about what you will and won't accept and how you wish to be treated. However, if Boomerang Boy is used to coming in and out of your life, hurting you and apologising each time, then perhaps it's worth asking yourself if he is really worthy of you.

"We teach people how to treat us."- Dr. Phil McGraw

Chapter 11: The Power of Forgiveness

Love Bless and Release

Sometimes we experience so much pain we find it difficult to let go. We find it difficult to forgive and move on, leaving us stuck in a negative cycle. However, it is we who are weighed down and filled with bitterness, resentment, anger, disappointment, and regret whilst whoever hurt you is walking around as light as a feather or perhaps continuing to treat others in the same hurtful way. Why are we carrying around their baggage? For hurt and pain are only inflicted as a result of other's insecurities. Ladies, why are we carrying these bags?! What's in the past is in the past and must stay there! Yes, this is easier said than done.

Sometimes we carry this burden—and believe you me, I've carried a heavy load for a long, long time (probably the cause of my back pain)—because we are afraid to let go. We may feel that if we let go, we are allowing the other person to "get away with it" or that we have become a "walkover" somehow by forgetting about it. But in essence what we are doing is quite the opposite; we are finally moving on without the load; without the negative thoughts and feelings eroding our backs, our emotions, and our Souls. We also may feel that we cannot let go as we become quite nostalgic about the past. The abuse or pain we endured becomes less "valid" if we let it go. It defines us in some way and we don't want to forget it. But in actual fact, what it's doing is making us move slower; it's making us weaker, bitter, and lonely. Let that traumatic and painful part of your journey not define you but serve as a tool to help you grow stronger and wiser, happier and lighter. Again easier said than done.

Remember, forgiving does not mean forgetting. It does not mean letting them back into your lives with the same circumstances—or at all, for that matter. It means seeing that person as a human being who's made some terrible mistakes but helped you grow in some way, whether it be emotionally, physically, mentally, or spiritually. For in every challenge or difficulty, strength and wisdom are to be gained. It means releasing that person and their negative energy and negative situation you endured from your own and freeing yourself. It means forgiving yourself for not feeling strong enough or wise enough to react or act differently at the time. Once forgiveness is achieved, we can finally take the next step to finding true happiness and Mr Right. Without forgiveness we will keep attracting the same circumstances, the same lessons, and the same type of person into our lives until forgiveness is learnt. I talk as a lady who's carried and dropped many bags in my lifetime!

"Forgiveness is the choice to see people as they are now. When we're mad at people, we're focusing on something they said or did before this moment. By letting go of the past, we make room for miracles to replace our grievances."-Miracle Cards- Marianne Williamson

"Forgive and forget all that has hurt you in the past and made you doubt your 'lovability.' Realise that hurt and disappointment are inevitable parts of our human learning experience. No matter how painful, the real injury was not that someone didn't cherish you, but that you erroneously believed you didn't deserve to be loved."-Soul Lessons and Soul Purpose Oracle Cards- Sonia Choquette.

Exercises to Try

Forgiveness, in most cases, does not happen overnight. Forgiveness takes time. Forgiveness is so very central to us living freer and lighter lives, but yet it can be one of the hardest things to do, especially in instances when we feel so very hurt, wounded, and aggrieved by another. Forgiveness may be the last thing we feel like doing. First, we must get ourselves in the position where we feel ready to want to start forgiving. Ask yourself, "Do I want to carry on feeling so bad, or do I want to move on with my life? Do I want to be full of resentment and carry this bitterness into my other relationships, or do I want to start afresh and convert these negative experiences into positive ones? Do I want to keep on attracting negative experiences because I am harbouring negative energy from a relationship that was unhealthy for me, or do I want to attract positive experiences into my life?" If you have answered the latter when considering these questions, then below are some exercises you can try to help with your forgiveness.

The Island Visualisation[1]

Imagine you are on an island. It's a beautiful island surrounded by an endless ocean of blue. The ocean is limitless. On this island there is just you and the person you are having difficulty with right out ahead of you at the front of the island. Gradually, very gradually, a light shines down from the sky, casting a brilliant white light over your island. The light is warm, and as you bask in it, you see it get thinner and thinner until it draws a bright

---

1 This visualisation (or similar) was taught to me and I use it continually

line across your island. As the light smiles back into the sky, you notice that the light has separated your island into two and that the front part of your island is slowly breaking away. Now, as you watch it ever so slowly break away and drift away from you, you begin creating.

Create anything you like on your island, for it is truly yours and only yours. Imagine the colours you would have it filled with, the sounds, the smells. You can put whatever and whomever you want on your island to come and join you. Have a party if you want, or you can keep the serenity and peace for you and you alone. It's your island to do whatever you want. As you create, also look out ahead of you and watch the part of the island that has separated from yours drift ... drift ... drift away.

You see the person you have chosen to free, standing, standing in their own power. Whatever they have done, whatever they have said is now forgiven. You have nothing but warm thoughts and good intentions towards this person as you watch them drift away and continue their own journey. You wish them love and you wish them peace. Put the past where it belongs in the past and send them away with love and kindness in your heart. As you watch them drift ... drift over the horizon, they are a mere dot in the ocean. You are full of peace. Now that they are out of your sight, you turn your attention towards your own island and feel an overwhelming sense of life, love, and laughter. You have never felt so free and alive. This life, this island is truly yours to treasure until the end of time. You are Light and you are Free. Stay for a few moments with this feeling. When you are ready, open your eyes.

Write a Letter

Write a letter to the person who has hurt you. Include all your thoughts and feelings—all the things you can and can't say. Don't hold back. Write it all down. If you are hurt, get it out. If you are angry, express it. When you have finished, get rid of the letter. You can burn it, throw it away, flush it down the toilet—just be sure to get rid of the letter.

The premise behind getting rid of the letter is that it represents getting rid of the pain the actions of this person has caused. It represents getting rid of our own baggage. If we choose to keep it in the house, we are keeping the negative energy of the past alive. We wouldn't have Post-it notes dotted around our house reminding ourselves of others' misguided actions inflicted upon us and hurtful words spoken against us, so why would we want a constant reminder of our hurt, pain, and anger? Why choose to keep that negativity in our psyche when you can make room for positive thoughts and feelings? Keep the closet clear! Are we going to read the letter over and over again to remind ourselves how angry and hurt that person made us feel? No. Forgive and get rid. As you get rid of the letter, repeat in your head the words, "I forgive you." Remember, forgiveness is powerful.

Make a List

Make a list of things that were said and done that caused you pain. Read over the list. Read the list again, and this time read it aloud and add the words "I forgive ..." before each line. For example, "I forgive you for cheating on me with XXX" or "I forgive you for not making time for me." As you read each sentence aloud, feel yourself becoming lighter and lighter as your pain and resentment ebb away.

Ask for Guidance

When in doubt, ask for guidance. There has been many a time I have found difficulty in forgiving somebody close to me, and I had to learn very quickly that some people in our life are there to stay, there to challenge us in some way. Although they may love us and although they may be an integral part of our lives, just as much as they offer positive qualities and experiences, they also present us with difficulties and challenges that require our constant forgiveness.

Forgiveness is not a one-off. It's a continual practise. Forgiveness does not discriminate. It does not say, "I've forgiven you once. That's your lot!" It says, "I forgive you" again and again. It also says, "I forgive me too for allowing this person into my life again to tread the same path" and "I forgive me for choosing to stay with a man who emotionally and physically abuses me." Remember, forgiveness also means forgiveness of Self. Forgiveness does not mean forgetting. Forgiveness does not mean allowing the same pattern to commence or inviting that person back into your life under the same conditions or even at all. It means forgiving the actions taken by that person and knowing that they were unable to know better at the time. It does not mean making excuses for them.

When you are struggling, ask for guidance. Whatever faith you believe in; whatever faith you do not believe in; whatever religion, culture, or ethnicity you are part of, whether you are atheist or agnostic, asking for guidance is something we can all do regardless of our beliefs.

Praying is a form of asking for guidance. It is a powerful way of surrendering our difficulties to God or a higher realm, a way of setting our intentions and having faith that they will be met.

Talking to friends; counsellors; relatives; wise, old elders; or spiritual leaders is a way of asking for guidance. Seeking advice through others who have shared the same experiences as you or can empathise with your experience, who can apply their own knowledge and objectivity on your situation, is a great way to step out of your own subjectivity and see the bigger picture.

Writing is also a way of asking for guidance. We can write down our thoughts in a letter, highlight our intentions, and have faith that in time our guidance will come. I find writing things on paper works very well for me.

I've had a very powerful experience happen to me once where I was walking home with a heavy heart. I'd been walking around like this for months, and I was becoming toxic with negativity, resentment, and underlying anger, yet I was still trying to put on my mask of happiness each morning. The cracks were showing as I was beginning to get ill with backaches, migraines, and an extremely stiff neck.

I had broken up with the love of my life just under a year before and still felt the residue of injustice and resentment imprinted all over me. He had done me wrong, and I felt as though he had got away with it. I remember seeking guidance from an elder at the time, and I remember them saying to me when talking about forgiveness, "I know that he's done you a disservice, and I know that you are hurting now, but if you did see him, is it more important to be right or to be kind?" At the time I protested that it wasn't about being right; it was about making him understand, but inside I heard myself screaming, "I don't want to be fricking kind! I'm sick of being KIND!!!!"

The thought of him walking around happy as Larry was getting me down. Why couldn't he realise just how cruel and selfish he had been? Why were my needs so unimportant and undervalued? Why did he make me feel so unworthy? Of course, if I hadn't felt unworthy myself, I wouldn't have been feeling these things at all. I would have seen that it was he who had felt unworthy and so had treated me this way. As I walked home with these thoughts playing like a broken record, my intuition told me to go to the park and sit down. "But I don't want to go to the blooming park. I want to go home!" I heard myself say inside. However, I am not foolish enough to ignore my intuition when it calls me, so I went to the park and sat down by this tree. As I sat down, I found two white feathers on either side of me. (White feathers have an extremely special significance to me, so I took this as a special moment.) I felt a sense of peace.

As I sat down, I had a feeling that for once and for all I had to let this man go. I knew that if I did not let this man go and if I did not forgive him, I would make myself a very ill woman indeed. Be under no illusion that this was easy for me. It simply was not. It was a last-chance call. A wake-up call for me. I had to get on with my life and find peace and a happy equilibrium within myself. As I sat under the tree, I closed my eyes and imagined him in front of me. I told him how I felt and why I felt that way; then I did the Island Visualisation. As I went home, I felt a little lighter and had a little more energy. With that extra energy I even wrote down my intention: "XXX and I will reach a peaceful and respectful understanding of each other's feelings, past and present. X will recognise any pain he may have caused, as will I. I want to put the past behind us and move forward into positivity and happiness. Please bring this to me! And So It Is!"

I wrote down this intention and put it under a small tea light. I lit the tea light and proceeded to get on with my evening. I had no expectations. No desperate feeling that this must happen, just a peaceful faith that at some point, when the time was right, it would happen. The very next day I got a phone call. Without me saying a word, he apologised for everything he'd ever done or said that had hurt me. I felt an overwhelming sense of peace and kindness in my heart, and from that day forward, I have been a huge believer in the power of forgiveness. The only thing that is true in this life is indeed Love. Nothing else is real.

Weeks before the park episode, I'd been asking for guidance through prayer, through meditation, and through speaking to friends. I knew I was in trouble and sinking fast and that I had to pick myself up. Through asking for guidance, whatever shape or form suits you, you are simply putting your intention out there. I had the guidance I needed to help me forgive fully, and for that I am so grateful! Gratitude also helps!

Gratitude

No matter how badly someone has treated us in the past, we can always find some positives. If we are still struggling to forgive, it is a good idea to start focussing not on what they have done wrong but on the things they have done right. Make a list of things they have done right or things they have done that have made you feel good. This not only raises your energy by focussing on the positive but also brings into your psyche feel-good thoughts and feelings associated with that person to counteract the negative, making them a far less toxic person in your mind. Before or after each positive sentence, write "I thank you." Look at the examples below.

I thank you for being a fantastic father to my children.

I thank you for supporting and encouraging me in my career.

I thank you for all the happy memories you helped me create.

I thank you for making me laugh when I was down.

I thank you for helping me through my relative's death.

I thank you for letting me wear your jacket even though you were freezing yourself.

There is so much power in gratitude and being grateful. We have so much to be grateful for—even through the dark times. Again, just because we write a list of positive things the person that has hurt us has done in the past, it doesn't mean we should suddenly forget what has happened and go back to them. What it does do is it balances out the negative. It helps us look objectively at this person as a whole, a multifaceted human being with many layers. It helps us connect with all that is good and do away with the toxic elements of the connection. It helps to be grateful for the experience we have had and makes room for more positive experiences in our lives.

Chapter 12: It's a Man's World (A Male Perspective)

We've heard from women all over the world discussing a universal theme: men and relationships. Writing a book like this, it is only fair to hear the other side of the story. Or as Men are from Mars and Women are from Venus suggests—the other side of the galaxy! Many men may see the title of this book and choose to act in a number of ways: some may immediately become defensive; some may shake their heads in dismay, saying, "Yes, I know plenty of those. They're always messing it up for us decent folk," and some men may try to rip the book down from the shelf for fear of being exposed.

But what about the brothers, fathers and uncles, who repeatedly witness their loved ones—sisters, daughters, and mothers—being mistreated over and over again by these unavailable men? How must it be to powerlessly witness another Mr Wrong bulldoze all over their lives? The urge to protect our own mothers, daughters, and sisters is strong amongst the male population, yet what I have discovered is that this is often forgotten once these same males begin playing the 'dating and relationship game.' It is often forgotten that these women are also somebody's daughter, sister, or mother.

It is often said that we are products of our childhood. That what we see, witness, and experience at the very early stages of our lives play a huge part in who we become. How many times have we met the stereotypical 'player' who replicates their absent father's ways? They grew up never wanting to be like him, yet years down the line, they finally open their eyes to see their own father staring back at them in the mirror. How many times have we seen the emotionally unavailable man who suffered some sort of loss, rejection, or abandonment in his formative years who is now unable to commit to a healthy relationship? The question we must ask ourselves is what is it about their stories that resonate with us so deeply that we keep wanting to get involved with them in the first place?

Are we as women too quick to brand these men "players," "cheaters," and "liars" without looking first within?

Can Mr Wrong Do a 360?!

Through listening to the experiences of ex 'players', 'bad boys', and 'Mr Wrongs', this chapter will attempt to answer the £1billion question. What is it that makes a Mr Wrong, and what role do women play in the creation? Some say that a leopard cannot change its spots, yet I believe that if the leopard changes the way that they perceive those spots, then the leopard can overcome all branding and therefore obstacles. If we look at the 'spots' as the blueprint of the man's life, why would or should this be changed? We all come with our belief systems, our conditionings, our stories, and our traits contained deep within our DNA. This is what makes us authentic. Instead of changing our stories from the past, we should look to use these stories as a vehicle to our success. Use our suffering and loss and abandonment to ensure that we become better people and therefore better partners to our loved ones. Change the way that these stories are perceived to build and enhance our lives and relationships with others. For it is not the stories or spots that make us who we are, but the way that we choose to use them. How must a man begin to change his story?

The following stories contain real life relationship experiences from a variety of men ranging from; Mr Wrongs to ex Mr Wrongs to Mr Nice guy fed up of paying the price for Mr Wrong. What impact is Mr Wrong having on men getting it right and are we so busy focussing on men that we fail to even see Mr Nice Guy?

Confessions of an Ex Mr Wrong

I think a good relationship should be built on mutual respect and support. Both parties should encourage each other in the right direction. Commitment to me means being there and making sure your partner and relationship are priorities. This means putting in 110% and putting the relationship first. As an ex-Mr Wrong I would have laughed this concept out of town!! Mutual respect? I wanted to bag as many beautiful girls as quickly as I could (unknown to them)—no strings, no fuss.

My first love was a 'false positive' in the sense that nothing else has ever quite matched up to that. I was only 13 years old. We met at school and were together for two years. It was everything I wanted in a relationship and actually want now. We were honest with each other, shared things with each other, and we'd talk all the time. ... We still speak now. To this day we have the same level of mutual respect and trust with each other. I eventually ended the relationship because one day I woke up and realised that I was more attractive than I thought I was. I was young and full of hormones and wanted to explore other opportunities and not be tied down.

I would definitely agree that there are a certain group of women who are attracted to "bad boys." Funnily enough, they always seem to be attracted to me but would always be bitterly disappointed. I used to be a "bad boy" or "player," shall we say, between the ages of 16-18, but at 33 years old I'm completely different now. I find the colder I am towards these types of girls, the more they begin to chase; however, when I start to defrost and let my natural guard down and my emotions out, they end up pulling away. I find it becomes a game of push and pull. It's almost as if they are used to noncommittal guys who push them away. I sometimes feel they enjoy the drama of being with someone who pushes them away—as if they have an urge to try and change them.

I would confess to being Mr Wrong. I was a terrible liar. I could never tell a girl the truth. I'd be like one of those idiots you see on The Jeremy Kyle Show. I would lie about everything: what I'd been doing that day, who I'd been doing it with, whether I was single or attached—you name it. I would say whatever it was I thought the girl wanted to hear. They were all short-term noncommittal relationships. Some girls would simply dump me, but I would still have six or seven on the go. I wouldn't be bothered, as I saw it as simply freeing up the calendar. I'd even call other girls by other names. This 'bad boy' phase lasted about two years. I was a bit of a late bloomer, and I think I felt like a kid in a candy store. I didn't have a lot of confidence growing up, and I guess I just wanted to use it to the maximum.

It was a combination of things that changed my way of thinking. I fell in love with someone whom I shouldn't have been with. She was in a relationship, but there was this mad connection. I didn't intend to fall in love with this person, but I did, even though I knew I could not have her. She made me reassess my way of thinking. I started to think about the other person's point of view. She herself was with somebody and unavailable, and this made me see the other side of the coin and how I was making these girls feel. It got to the point where I looked in the mirror and didn't like what I saw. I began to think about how I might feel if somebody treated my mother or one of my many sisters this way. I was at the point where friends would regard me as the 'bad boy' who couldn't be trusted and would never introduce me to female friends or relatives. In fact they would warn them against me! I started to ask myself, 'Would this make my mum proud? Is that how she raised me? Is this how I want to be known?' The answer was No, so I set out changing that.

James, 34, London, England

Mr Workaholic

I'm 42 and unmarried. I have so many regrets in my life. The biggest regret of my life is losing my Soul Mate Amanda. Amanda was such a beautiful, intelligent, and independent woman. I still remember her laugh, her smile, and all the love and support she showed me. I was running my own business at the time. I met Amanda while I was an estate agent and gradually worked my way up to a property developer. We began dating properly when I began setting up my own business. Although I loved being with Amanda, I felt I had something to prove, so I worked and worked myself into the ground. Six months into our relationship, I was working 60, 70, and sometimes 80-hour weeks. She eventually got sick of me working all the time. She felt I never had time for her and that I chose to work rather than to spend time with her. I simply could not understand why she was not understanding of my situation.

We broke up for six months and I missed her terribly. Instead of picking up the phone, I worked harder and longer. Because my business was doing so well, I did not recognise the ache in my heart until I bumped into her by accident. She was with another man, and I felt a massive stabbing pain in my heart I had never felt before. We exchanged numbers as her sister was looking for someone to help with her property. We began talking again and it was as if we had never broken up.

Three months later we began dating again and things took a turn rapidly. I knew this was my last chance. She explained to me how taken for granted she felt and how quality time and building memories was important to her. For a while, I gave her the world: my love, my attention, and most importantly, my time. We moved in, and she became pregnant soon after. I was still working long hours but tried to give her the support she needed. I always felt like it was never enough as she would complain that I worked during the weekends, that I jumped whenever my phone rang, and that we never did things together anymore. I wondered why she couldn't see that all this working was for her and our son.

Once the baby was born, I felt redundant once again. I felt that I could never do anything right and had trouble bonding with him as well as Amanda. It was as though I had put all my energy into work, and I didn't know how to switch off. I would be so tired I would often flop onto the couch and fall asleep, which she would always disapprove of and accuse me of not supporting her. It didn't occur to me that being a mother was a full-time job.

I tried hard to change things as I could see how much it was hurting her. She became withdrawn and cold and would spend nights at her sisters. I felt pushed out and threw myself into working extra hours and became even more unavailable. I loved Amanda to bits, but I didn't know how much I was hurting her. I guess I felt pushed out. I understand now why she burst into tears when I organised a celebratory meal and drink with my team. I understand why she swore at me when I chose to go on a stag weekend with the boys. I had forgotten to see her as a partner—the woman I loved—and had begun seeing her as the woman who nagged me when I got home. It was easy and hassle free to go out with the boys I managed. At no point during the first year and a half of our baby's life did I think to ask her out with me.

I remember her crying and telling me that she couldn't do this anymore. She was tired of being second fiddle to my work, to my friends, and everything else. For the first time, I looked in her eyes, and I acknowledged the pain I had put her through. I realised then I had let my own inadequacies and need to prove and gain approval take over and ruin the beautiful bond we had between us.

It was too late and I will always love Amanda. I know I can never get her back. She moved on very quickly and is now happily married to a man who can give exactly what I couldn't: his time. I still see my son and have learnt that quality time is what makes a relationship.

After counselling, I realised that I still carried feelings of worthlessness and inadequacy I felt when my father left. Since then, I had always been trying to prove I was a success. Recognising this was not enough; it took losing Amanda to realise what was truly important. I now have all the time in the world for my son and would sacrifice work over him in a heartbeat. I've learnt that time will not stand still for anyone. Do I want to look back at my life and be filled with memories of work, targets, and goals, or be filled with memories of love, joy, and laughter?

David, 42, Toronto, Canada

Mr Dreamer Speaks Out!

I feel great being single most of the time. I feel free as I can do whatever the hell I want, whenever I want, however I want. It is great to flirt with girls and to be around them as I love female company (sometimes more so than male). I think the reason for this is that they are nice to look at, and there is always a chance something may happen. Also, you can be more honest with girls about stuff, and it's great to be able to be in charge of the conversation. With men, they like to fight for control of the group.

I usually start wanting a relationship when I meet a girl I like. I become my best self, which is little more than an act. I will try to be the most perfect person she wants me to be with the sole intention of getting her into bed. And, after the sex, my thought process goes along the lines of, 'That was enjoyable. I would like to get this sex on tap. I would like to show this girl a good time, whisk her off her feet, and show her how much of a nice guy I am.' Usually the girl genuinely makes me feel like this, but it is short-lived and I have set the standard way too high for myself so that it is impossible to live up to. For example, I will buy flowers for her for no reason, I will say 'I love you' way too early for the sole reason that it feels good when ladies say it back, I will cancel plans with my mates and say I prefer hanging out with her anyway, I will keep my house tidy or offer her a place to leave stuff, I will listen with interest about her problems and talk them over with her. I will kill them with kindness and selfless acts.

All this will make her think I am great. Then, usually after about six months, I revert back to being my selfish self. I say 'revert', but 'regress' would probably be more apt.

This would be fine, as I am usually a nice person, just not as nice as I am in those first stages, but because I set the bar so high early on, it looks like I am losing some of the love I had in the past. This will cause arguments such as, 'You don't love me anymore' or 'You used to do special things for me', etc. I set the bar far too high and then fail to live up to her now-high expectations.

Then I will want to do something, and I won't be able to because I have to think about someone other than me and that will drive me crazy, so we will break up.

Don't get me wrong—at the start, I like doing all the relationshippy things but then they become chores. Going to see parents is a pain in the arse. I know it is a cliché, but in-laws are always a nightmare. People don't think your parents are as great as you do.

Day trips—at first, these are great as you get to know each other and all the stories we tell are new and interesting. We can have fun as we are showing off how fun and exciting we are, and we can because we have the drug-like buzz of being in a new relationship. Over time though, we run out of interesting things to say at dinner, you have heard all our jokes, and the conversation becomes mundane and repetitive: 'How was your day? What do you want for dinner? How is your mum? We need to pay this bill.'

When the talking goes, the sex is not far behind. Behind every attractive girl, there is a bloke bored of sleeping with her. We men like variety, and to be fair, even bad sex is usually good. It is usually the woman who, before your very eyes, stops being a radiant sex goddess and slowly becomes someone who nags you and stops you from doing things, and who never initiates sex any more.

Get-out clauses I use to get out of these relationships are: I become distant, go out more often, and stop the romantic gestures. I know this sounds arse-hole-ish, but relationships really do become a chore. I yearn for my singledom, even if I am deeply in love. I want to go and sit in a pub all day. I want to watch an entire box set of 24. I want to play poker or football manager all night. I don't want to do the dishes 'right now'.

I feel really bad when it finally ends because it is not the girl's fault. It is me setting myself up to fail at the end. It really is hard to fathom that I will be in a long, committed relationship for long as this is a cycle I cannot seem to break.

If I could take my own advice, I would try looking at an old partner with new eyes rather than getting a new partner. This would save lots of time and heartache. Looking at someone in a new way could bring back those feelings you had at the start of a relationship. Also whenever I am drunk, I become very 'rose-tinted' and long for the girls that I have lost. Sometimes I get them back and the cycle starts again. I will say I have changed and be all romantic again, and as soon as I get her back, I become selfish again.

I don't want to settle for anything less than perfection, and I usually find it, but it quickly fades.

At my age, you start contemplating a family, but I am not grown up enough for one yet and I am far too selfish—although I think it is better to wait until I am ready rather than doing it because everyone else is and put a poor girl through hell just because I rushed into it.

My advice to women is that they need to put a higher value on sincerity over romance. Would you rather have frequent romantic gestures from someone who may have cheated on you, or someone that is not romantic but is always honest and well behaved? On the subject of romance, I think it devalues the more times you do it. One of my friends bought his girlfriend flowers every week. He used to get a lot of sex and praise for this, but because he has done it for so long, it is routine and she doesn't even appreciate them anymore as she is used to them.

Another tip for women is men need space. More than space, men need to know that they are appreciated. Seriously, if we do something nice, even if it is expected of us, tell us we are doing a good job. Praise our muscles or intellect or handiness and do it in front of people. You will be amazed at how far it goes!

I would definitely say I am a Mr Dreamer when it comes to women as I always promise the world. Or I talk about getting married and having kids when I doubt it will happen in the near future. I wouldn't call this a lie though, as when I say it, I genuinely mean it in that moment, but it will be fleeting.

I don't think I will change unless I get a personality transplant, or even just grow up a little. I like sex with a variety of girls too much to ever sacrifice it for one girl. I have fantasies of having kids and being a good dad quite often, but I don't want to go through the relationship before and after to have one. Maybe I'll adopt as a single dad (Dreamer again).

My advice to other Mr Dreamers is to set the bar lower at the beginning and try to raise it as the relationship progresses rather than the other way around. Advice that I can give (but not take myself) is don't get too far into a relationship if you know it won't last and you just fancy a shag. And finally, be up front and honest with women if you are just after a one-week stand.

Adam, 27, Manchester, England

My Girlfriend from Hell

I really hate my (ex) girlfriend. She has got worse over the last month, and I just sent her a text to tell her our relationship is over. I cannot stand her behaviour anymore. We have just grown apart; we want different things from life. I want to build an empire, and she is happy drinking cocktails in Westfields.

My girlfriend said at the beginning of our relationship that she needs a man ready to commit, to share her life with. She wanted to be married, buy a house in Essex, and own a couple of businesses. Neither of us are big fans of working for other people. Here I am, ready to commit; however, as soon as it is time to start saving and put the hard work in, it is like I am on my own because my thinking is too expansive.

The first two months we were together we spent night and day in each other's company. We worked on the same team at Scotland Yard. Due to our working schedule, we kept our relationship a secret. It was normal to date another police officer because of the shift hours we worked. It would be challenging to be with someone who works a normal nine-to-five as we wouldn't see each other regularly. One night I went to visit her. We both had our own flats; she lived in Camden West London and I lived in Lewisham South London. That night turned into a month. In those 30 days, that is when our heaven turned into hell.

After two weeks in her flat, she started to criticise me every day: "You are not organized. You are stupid. That's not the proper way to do this or that." Then one day she told me, "You're just a small boy in the force. You should be happy to be with a higher ranking officer." I felt hurt and belittled.

I thought to myself, why does she stay with me then? If I am not good enough for her, what was the point? I felt that whatever I did was never good enough for her and believe me—I have tried so much to save our relationship. I even surprised her by taking her out to the cinema, and then we ate at a restaurant. I even put myself out of pocket as I tried to be the man she wanted!

Apart from seeing her at work, I would give her space to do her own thing, trying every strategy I could think of: I tried taking sick days off work when I was not sick; I was being nicer than usual; I threatened to leave her then I tried to talk to her. We even had a session with a friend of ours who is a relationship coach, but she always played the perfect partner when our friends from outside work were around. However, after they left, she would start to ignore me again.

Everything that was wrong with our relationship was always my fault! Every mistake, every fight. However, this was not the truth of the situation. I am not mad. I can recognise my responsibilities; however, she was not able to do the same. I hate her. She makes me feel like a piece of trash or a monster. I think she enjoyed playing with my feelings and trying to manipulate me.

I would ask her if she loved me and the answer would always be "yes," so why she behaved like that I will never know. A part of me now feels she wanted more attention or more power. I think she was trying to drive me insane. She never showed her love to me. Why did she stay with me? Every day I would wake up in this love soap. I feel insecure because she shows me no love and makes me very jealous. I even have nightmares of her cheating on me, and it actually caused more fights. Our relationship was a vicious cycle. I tried to explain to her a thousand times what I need from her to be happy, and she was not trying to put any effort. I do not know why she kept me hanging like this.

I wanted to leave her, but I didn't want to meet someone else and have to start the process of getting to know each other all over again, only to find out they're just the same or worse. I thought I might as well stick with the problems I have and try to fix them. It is not just that I didn't have the guts to do so but because I had a very soft spot for her in my heart. Moreover, I am love dependant as I did not grow with my parents telling me they loved me. I fall in love easily and most times with the wrong people; sometimes I feel I am a "bird in a cage." I wanted to leave her, but I couldn't pluck up the courage to phone her and tell her. I told her while crying and eating popcorn that I wanted to end it as it was not working out and we have been growing apart for a while now. I was almost begging her to "set me free". I told her this relationship was destroying me and she said, "Calm down now. We will talk about this tomorrow. Kiss kiss, goodnight, love you, hun." That was just a way to keep me quiet. The next day she did not call me.

I could not take it anymore and by lunchtime, I stupidly sent a text and she answered with, "I'll call you after lunch, hun." She did not. I called her before she left work as I was on football guard duties. She replied and said she could not talk because she was in a meeting. I sent a text later that night to answer my question about what I had asked. No reply. I was crushed. I sent another text and still no answer. I tried to call. Nothing. My jealousy took over me and drove me crazy. I started daydreaming about another man around her flat and the two of them looking at my missed calls and laughing. I sent her a text and I said, "It's over!" I cannot stay with a woman who is not able to answer a text probably because she is too busy.

I hate this woman. She is wrong for me and I wish I had never met her. I thought she was great at the beginning and that she wanted to commit to me. I was in heaven and I have invested so much in this relationship. I thought for once she was "The One." We worked together for five years before crossing the line as lovers. She promised me so much and delivered so little with her emotional unavailability. Now, here we are between a big rock and a cold, metal, hard place.

Although I may hate her now, I know in time I will love again. This experience has taught me that I must love myself first, and although I am a loving man, I must not let others take advantage of me. I think men get a bad rap. Whilst there are men who mistreat women, this experience has shown me that there are many Miss Wrongs out there too!

Gwenton Sloely, 28, London, England

The Science of Relationships

You can't have a successful relationship until you know what you're doing. You need to court so you can find out who they are and where they're at. You also need to know who you are and who are dealing with. Most of us jump into relationships out of need. We look at the superficial things, like 'She looks good. I'll have a bit of that.'

A relationship means 'relating to,' so you need to know exactly what you are 'relating to.' We should look at our past experiences to work out what has and hasn't worked and why in order to create a relationship that is meaningful. Commitment means following an order. It's a series of things you need to do consistently to ensure the growth of the relationship. For example, if you are a

Christian, you follow the order: you pray, fast, read Scripture to show commitment to your faith. It's the same in a relationship. In saying this, you need to know what you are committing to. It's like buying a phone or a car. You may not like the phone after a two-week trial. You may have to take the car for a test drive before you commit. Get to know them. Have a trial period. You can't commit to what you don't know. You can commit only once you know what you are committing to.

Your first experience of love is with your mother and father. You carry that into your relationship. What you see and experience growing up has a great impact into how you carry yourself and your ideas about love into any romantic relationship. I didn't get into a relationship until I was 16. I liked her more than she liked me. The experience taught me to be careful. It was short-lived and lasted only a month or two. She was in a vulnerable place and I was more stable. I find that women who are vulnerable or needy are more receptive. I used to go down to all the places like Trocerdero, Moonshot, and Brixton to 'chirpse'[1] and I met her in Trocerdero . I would go and see her in her hostel and creep back home late at night. I had a lot to give then. I still do. When a man really likes a woman, he will give and give. He will give his time and energy. Now though, I do not give too much too soon because what is there to look forward to?

A first date should not be about impressing a woman; it should be about getting to know them.

When it comes to dating, we will test you. If you 'give it up' too soon, we will not commit to you. We will get bored. Men are natural warriors and hunters. Look at The Clash of the Titans. Before he could marry her, he had to go through a series of trials and tribulations. This creates a sense of value and worth.

---

1 Sl: chat up

I speak for most men when I say this: once we get into a relationship and get hurt, we so often jump into another relationship or 'situation' and don't really care. We may get into a relationship where the woman likes you more than you like them. Unintentionally, we may end up getting into something we are not ready for. So many men end up meeting all these lovely people who are ready to commit and we can't. We are creatures of Love. From the day we are born, we yearn for Love. It doesn't matter how hard it's been or that we haven't given ourselves time to heal; people come into our lives and we want that love but we are not ready.

It's so important for us in relationships to do our homework on each other. What do we know about this person? Do we know about their past history or if they're ready to commit? We allow ourselves to get caught up in lust, and it often becomes one imbalanced mess. We need to get to know the person. Again, it's like buying a car. We don't just buy the car. We get to know the service history of the car. The older the car, the more users it's had. How many registered keepers has it had? If it's had so many registered keepers, then what is wrong with the car that someone keeps selling it on? Somewhere along the lines, the car must be broken.

I have been a Mr Wrong in the past. I have promised my woman things that have never materialised. For example, I have promised that we would do this and do that but it would never happen. The intention was there but it just didn't happen. There was a period of time I used to cheat. I was with a woman and I cheated on her twice. She didn't find out. I cheated on her because I felt something was missing in the relationship. I had no legitimate reason to cheat but I did. Her ex was still around, and I felt they still had a connection so I suppose I used that as an excuse to do my thing. Looking back, I wished we'd courted and we'd got to know each other better. I hadn't fully committed to her. If I had, I would have got to know who she was. Commitment also means getting to know myself and my fears. If we can't speak and be truly open and honest with each other, then something is missing.

I have come across women who are jaded and paint all men with a negative brush. Women like this have clearly been hurt. These women, I feel, are the ones who crave love the most. Most women like that have not healed properly and haven't understood or loved themselves properly and so they project it outwards, saying, "You men this and you men that!" It becomes a vicious cycle. Whatever you think, you bring about. If you focus on prosperity, you will get it. Programming is key. A lot of girls now are surrounded by women, aunties, mothers, and sisters who berate and beat men down with, "All men are … All men are …." It's important to not shove our own personal and negative experiences on our younger generation. What we need to teach our children is the Science of Mating, The Science of Relationships, and The Science of Loving Ourselves.

Again when or if we enter relationships with these types of jaded women, we need to ask ourselves pertinent questions. Going back to my car analogy, these are the questions we must consider. Were there any crashes caused by the driver? What is the long-term damage? Is it worth it? Can you fix it? The number one person you need to protect is yourself. You can't have someone messing with your heart. It only causes hurt, depression, and a sense of low self-esteem. You should be your first Love.

Courtney, 37, London, UK

My Ex Used To Do THAT!

A key indicator of a successful relationship is honesty. Transparent, open and clear communication is essential. Sometimes being transparent leaves us feeling vulnerable, however both parties need to able to express that vulnerability for a successful relationship. For men, it can be especially difficult because of the pressures in society. It's becoming increasing difficult to appear vulnerable and not "lose face" as a man.

We are taught that we need to be tough, resilient and have a hard outer shell. I notice this in my own life and experience. The truth is it's hard out there for a guy! We are expected to know so much and have as few faults as possible and of course this conflicts with the need to be weak or vulnerable which naturally draws us closer to our other half.

Honesty is important even if the truth hurts. It builds a firm foundation. Friendship is key too. Without friendship, again, there is no foundation. I had to learn this. When I was young, it was all about the "hips, the lips and the fingertips" but now I realise that there needs to be a long term friendship before any intimacy can take place.

Commitment, to me, means honouring a responsibility and agreeing to be responsible or accountable for the relationship, it's a contract and there are terms and conditions. When you enter into a commitment, it's a responsibility. In terms of a relationship, it's about knowing who you are committing to and taking responsibility. This means being held accountable when things go wrong as well as if they are going well.

In my own work with children and families, I have witnessed the impact of lustful relationships. As men, we get caught up in the aesthetics, the outer shell and the outer appearance. I have two children from two separate relationships. I love my children and thank God for them. This experience, along with becoming Christian, has taught me a lot about me and how I saw the world. After having had two children, I now have a better appreciation of what 'partnership' means and what love means. My outlook has changed dramatically.

Love is about surrendering yourself and living for that other person. We are taught to be quite selfish and, like many other men, instead of seeing women as potential partners I got caught up in "the lips, hips and fingertips." Society projects these values and I followed. True love is patient, nurturing and empowering. I have been on dates — and I mean a lot of dates — and it can only be a good thing! You really get to gain an understanding of the complex creatures that women are! I mean, I have been on dates where my date was petrified of ordering food (perhaps shyness or nerves). I was like "Are you going to eat that because I will" she did need to put on some weight though, but now I hear she is happily married and I saw a Facebook photo of her recently—she could have been easily mistaken for Queen Latifah! My point is I guess different people unlock different parts of us but we need to truly know ourselves and be comfortable with those rough edges before we start getting familiar with the opposite sex.

I remember dating another lady who couldn't help but tell me that I reminded her of her ex. When I ate I would hear, "My ex ate like that," if I laughed or cracked a joke "my ex used to do that," if I excused myself to go toilet "My ex used to do that" and whenever she would say that there would be an unsettling twitch in her right eye (you know, a bunny boiler look). As I am sure you can tell we

didn't have a third date but I really learnt something from that—
stay away from internet dating! But more importantly, we need to
get over our past hurts and heal before we can embark on our next
adventure.

You have to realise I have been fortunate to have God bless me
with an exceptional mother who passed away when I was 18. Even
though I only had her in my life for a short time, we had such a
powerful and close relationship. She was the benchmark for what
a woman should be. Perhaps subconsciously I look for women who
share the same values as my mum: someone who is maternal, caring
and affectionate as well as someone who has integrity and loyalty.
So I went from high expectations to the Mike Tyson right hook of
reality!

Although my first experience of a woman – my mum – was
positive, having a child in my first relationship really threw me. I
was in a relationship when I was very young, 16, and the girl I was
with became pregnant. I was scared at the time and didn't know
what to do but part of me was happy. On reflection, at 16 what do
you know about becoming a parent? You are literally a child yourself
with a life full of experiences ahead of you and it's abruptly cut short
by a new responsibility. I could only imagine what this was like for
my girlfriend at the time. I can understand her parents, on the other
hand, were furious, the impact of being a teenage parent, coupled
with the relationship breakdown and the animosity of the maternal
family pushed me further away from my daughter. My girlfriend's
dad wanted to kill me! Not having any experience in court litigation
and parenthood I had no recourse to challenging this process, pretty
much the reality of many men today. I have battled in courts ever
since to be a part of my children's life. This experience has, of course,
affected my relationships as I have spent a lot of time battling in
courts trying to enforce a right that should be inherent upon the

birth of a dependent. It's been a hard road but one I am committed to. I have committed myself to this cause and have even set up a company to help other fathers to understand their parental rights and support the family following separation and family breakdown. This has been therapy for me, being able to effectively make a positive impact on other families in place of my denied relationship with my own children. To be fair, even as I write this I am starting to question how I have continued to fight for so long, it is truly amazing and I give God the praise and glory!

This issue of family breakdown, divorce and separation is an important one. It really frustrated me to learn that both my son and daughter were being raised by other men and I have been totally shut out of the process! Why would any woman want to allow another man to raise their children knowing full well that their natural father is out there wanting to play his part? Sheer bitterness and anger I guess. This current family law system makes it relatively easy for a man to walk out on his family; in fact, I would argue that it promotes it, based on the benefit/ welfare system in the UK alone. However, because it is so easy for a man to leave the family it makes it even easier to push him out of the picture altogether!

I have always wanted to be present in the lives of my children and I have been in court regarding my son for most of his life. He will be 11 this year and we started proceedings before his 2nd birthday, disgusting really that it has been allowed to drag on for so long and what for? Because the relationship ended and I chose to honour my role as a father and accepted the ending of a relationship? In all honesty, my son is being made to pay for what are ultimately adult issues and the current law system allows such injustices to take place. The situation gets even more intense when you consider the Child Support Agency; it seems they view all fathers in a deficit model. How can we support a system that pushes for the financial accountability of fathers but turns a blind eye to the injustice of the denied physical and emotional presence of a father? I believe it sends a very clear message that fathers aren't important but we will have your MONEY!

This is the first time that I have been able to pen my feelings, my thoughts, my story! I am sure there are a lot of Mr Wrongs out there and indeed a lot of Ms nutcases (believe me I have met them), but there are always two sides to a story accompanied by a baggage load of past hurts and bad experiences. My intention to share this story is an opportunity for people to learn, in particular women, about their decisions and choices within relationships. It is not right for a child to be used as a weapon in order to achieve some ill gained advantage over your ex-partner or to smear his name amongst his friends, families and networks. Some men need to equally take responsibility and handle their business; forget chasing the cars, big houses and material things, what is material is your relationship with your God given gift, your child.

I think women who are hung up on Mr Wrong need to forgive but not forget. Forgiveness will help them to heal. Each Mr Wrong needs to be seen as a lesson. Everything bad that happens helps us learn and grow. When you get hung up and bitter it ages you; mutual family friends have expressed how the constant battling and court antics have taken their toll on my ex. It's best to let it go of the bitterness for your own sanity. Some women are so hung up on Mr Wrong that, when they do meet Mr Right, they simply do not recognise him and that is a damn shame.

Julian, 33, East London, England

Mr Nice Guy Pays the Price

Communication is key in a relationship. Even if you don't necessarily agree on anything, it's understanding the other point of view and respecting it. Doing things together is really important as well. It should be "we not me." Commitment to me means loyalty, being there for the long haul, ideally forever. It's being with that person no matter the difficulties, through the ups and downs, the good and the bad. The biggest turnoffs for me in a woman are vanity, selfishness, and women who don't consider or listen to the other person in the relationship.

My first experience of love was when I was 18. Her name was Leila. I was in love, we were good friends, but we never went out. I was so into her. She invited me to her 18th birthday party. Her boyfriend was there. I remember it shocked me. It broke my heart. When I asked her about him, she insisted that she'd told me she had a boyfriend but unfortunately I didn't recall. It is possible she did, and perhaps I was so wrapped up in her it didn't register in my head. Although we weren't together, I felt crushed and somehow betrayed.

My second experience of love was 13 years ago. I was 21 and coming home from Uni one day when I spotted this cute girl on the train. JayCee was giving me lots of suggestive eye contact and I asked for her number. We started going out, but I noticed after a while she seemed paranoid. Every time I hugged her in public she would make excuses, saying her brother might see her. I thought this was a bit weird, but the relationship carried on for nearly a year this way. After a while, I noticed she became a bit distant. I got a phone call one day from her. She was emotional and sad. Her friend had introduced her to a guy and she felt torn between us. I was confused as to why her friend would introduce them knowing we were going out, but I told her that the choice was hers and that she must make a decision. A few days later I saw her walking hand in hand with him. I felt crushed.

A few years later JayCee messaged me on Facebook through a friend's account I didn't recognise. It turned out that the man she'd left me for was controlling and emotionally abusive and monitored her Facebook usage. She told me she still loved me, but she also still loved her 'bad boy.' I later found out that she had two children with this man. She eventually broke up with him as he was too controlling. We ended up at the same party together and all my friends warned me NOT to go there again. I didn't.

It wasn't long until he moved back in with her and I found myself in the position of giving her relationship advice. I was telling her to take it slowly, to have the relationship more on her terms. During this time I was still single and had feelings for her, but I was the 'nice friend' who helped her in her difficult relationship.

Both experiences have affected me in the sense that I learnt that it is good to keep your options open. I feel like I've developed a defence mechanism whereby I would talk to other girls as friends, knowing that if my girlfriend left me I wouldn't be left alone. I didn't want to experience the hurt of being left alone again.

After this I became 'involved' with another girl, Kyla. We worked together. I really liked her and she really liked me. She had a five-year-old and wasn't looking for any type of commitment or loyalty. She certainly wasn't committed or loyal, but she glossed over it as if it had nothing to do with me. We were 'good friends.' We would kiss and hug and share our problems, but it never became more than that. All our work colleagues would say we were like girlfriend and boyfriend, but we would look at each other and say we were just friends. However, we became close, and I met her mum and she loved me straight off! She loved me like a son. She would always keep asking, "When are you marrying my daughter?" I'd even met her granddad and brothers and they really made me feel like part of the family.

Kyla would always ask me for things. Could I get her this, could I get her that? I liked her so much I would get it for her. I felt so attracted to her, and her son loved me too. However, she also had a neighbour who loved her. He also paid for her phone contract, and I later found out that another guy from another department at work had also paid for her phone contract. Yet I would get her all sorts—help with her phone contract, pay for this, pay for that. I even paid for her job on a cruise ship, which messed me up money-wise. I was so blinded—I just wanted to help her. However, I began to realise that I was doing so much and started to question what she did for me. This went on for three years and it never moved past the kissing and hugging stage. Although we weren't physically intimate, there was a definite connection and her playing around began to feel like a betrayal.

One day, a colleague's friend asked her for her BB pin, and she gave it to him, right in front of me. We would argue and she would say, "We're not in a relationship!" It felt like a big disrespect. Despite this, I would still message and call her. The experience with Kyla really messed me up in a big way, yet I continued pursuing her. Eventually, it all ended. She said it never went any further because I wasn't at the right stage in my life. I didn't have my own car or my own place.

Looking back, she had a lot of baggage. Her dad left her when she was a teenager, and she supported the father of her child financially, even while she was pregnant. To thank her for her support and for carrying and mothering his child, he upped and left her when the child was young. He felt emasculated as she was the protector and *provider of both her partner and son. He would send a card perhaps once a year but would not contribute financially or get involved in the child's life. When I met her, she was still going through the effects of this. Perhaps I was Mr Nice Guy, feeling the effects of a woman who had been done wrong.*

I think Mr Wrong has messed it up for the good guys out there. I do also think that Mr Nice Guys can also turn into Mr Wrongs because they experience so much crap. My experiences have made it hard to trust. In the back of my mind, I think even if they appear good or innocent, they still might have another man on the go or cheat. I remember saying to Kyla once, "I'm going to go and sleep around with lots of women," and I remember her saying, "Don't ever change yourself. You're nice." But I can understand why so many 'nice guys' change because it gets to the point where I think if something's not going well in your life, then something's got to change. Perhaps the question we need to ask ourselves is, is it is we that need to change or the type of women we choose to date?

John, 34, London, England

Why I Could Never Be a Mr Wrong

I think what makes a successful relationship is communication and not just thinking about yourself but the relationship as a whole. It's like starting a business—you have to think about the desired result. When I went into my relationship, I went into it saying this is the girl I want to marry, so no matter what problems came in between us, I would focus on the end result. I call it having a vision for the relationship. Commitment is an important factor too; it means dedication, focus, consistency, and being able to communicate.

Commitment means dedicating your time, your effort, and your energy into the relationship or person. My biggest turnoff, when it comes to women, is women who swear, smoke too much, have bad attitudes, and love to complain. There is a difference between women who talk sense and women who just complain. I can't bear it. I'm a positive guy.

The first time I fell in love was a great experience. I couldn't believe how it felt. It made me feel better about myself. I couldn't believe that someone I loved actually loved me back! It made me feel confident and happy. I was 15 years old and she was my next-door-neighbour's cousin. I'd always look out my window at her when she played in the garden. I asked about her and we eventually got chatting one day. Finally I asked her out. I used to write her love letters. This was way back before we used mobile phones or sent text messages or friend requests! I would include little love hearts and tell her I liked her. After the fourth letter I told her I loved her, and she responded back telling me she loved me too! It was all very teenage. We'd kiss and hold hands. I didn't feel scared. I instantly told her I felt the same way whenever she told me she loved me. We went out for 14 months. Communication was hard as we didn't have mobile phones, and although we both lived in South London, it felt like it was long distance! It naturally fizzled out. My memories of my first love are very positive, and because it was my first experience, it was very memorable.

It has affected me in the fact that I'll never forget the hurt when she ended the relationship. Despite the fact that what she was saying was the truth, I didn't want to accept it. I now don't pour out my feelings immediately like I used to for fear of being hurt. I have also become more stubborn in the sense that if a girl ends a relationship with me, I act nonchalant.

From what I've been told, I can be very stubborn and I also don't always express my feelings. I always thought that women wanted a bad boy, so for a while I tried to become one but it didn't quite work out for me. The meanest I ever got was saying "No" to women instead of "Yes" all the time. I could have been a Mr Wrong if I wanted to, but if my father had found out I was ever to be the kind of son who'd been sleeping with five or six girls at a time, he would have killed me. I can actually hear him bellowing, "Michael, remember the name that you carry!" For that reason alone I could never be a Mr Wrong. My mother who gave me life would take it back. Believe!

Michael, 30, London, England

Mr Wrong Messin' It Up for the Rest of Us!

My first love is not a heartbreak story. I met her at college. She sent me a Valentine's letter card in our college Valentine's mail. We got together quite soon after that, and we dated for two or three years. I felt like I wasn't allowed to have a girl this beautiful. I was head over heels for her. I took her out and treated her the way I would love to be treated. I gave her everything she needed and put her first. I even put her needs above mine and made compromises in order to keep the relationship happy. In turn, she did the same for me. After a while, we stopped doing things together and we grew apart. As a result, the relationship fell apart, and we both went our separate ways to respective Universities. It was a mutual thing. We are still very good friends to this day. Soon after she went to University, she met a man and got married. I sometimes still think to this day that that could have been me, but I am happy for her.

I dated a girl five years younger than me. She was at University, and I was chasing my career and trying to achieve my dreams. We were both at different stages in our lives. I was struggling to achieve my dreams and she was exploring a new world at University. The relationship was exciting at first, and we would bounce ideas off each other. However, I needed support and she wasn't able to offer it to me. It made our relationship difficult to manage. I felt she was selfish, and I stopped wanting to talk to her about my issues as she was not understanding and was often negative when I needed support. We ended up arguing a lot and having an on-off relationship. The strain began taking its toll on the relationship. I loved her to bits, but I knew I had to make a decision. It was the hardest decision to make, but the pain outweighed the love I felt. When the bad outweighs the good, then the good was no longer enough. It was heart-breaking.

She moved on a week later and began dating someone else. It was like my world had been turned upside down. I'd never experienced this before. I was devastated. The only way I can describe it was it felt as though I was on a constant rollercoaster looking down just before it descended. I felt it physically. I had butterflies in my stomach. It was constant. I'd have it all day; I'd go to bed with this nauseating feeling in my stomach and wake up with it. I wasn't eating because of it, and I constantly felt sick. It took a while to get back, but luckily I had great friends around me for support. I have a lot of female friends, and I found talking to them a great help. I would never talk to my male friends about things like this. It's not the 'done' thing. I'm a guy. We have to keep face and be a man. I knew if I tried to talk to them, they just wouldn't understand. A woman can see things from the female perspective. I have learnt that men and women can see things very differently. Talking to my female friends gave me insight, and at times, confirmation I needed.

I spoke to her a while after this on and off. She said that the new guy was just a distraction and that everyone deals with things in different ways. She wanted me back a while after, but I could never take her back. I could never go through feeling like that again. You only get one chance.

I know lots of Mr Wrongs. At least 99% of my friends are Mr Wrongs. They have girlfriends, and their girlfriend is almost like their safety net. They stay at their girlfriend's house or may even live with them, but they go out at night to clubs and act single. They pull girls and sleep with them and go back home like it never happened. I personally don't know why or how they do it. It's annoying. They mess it up for me because all the other girls think I am like that, and I end up picking up the pieces.

I met a girl recently and have begun dating her. She recently broke up with her fiancé who slept with someone else and got her pregnant. They had been together for about four years, so the relationship was pretty serious. She is so vulnerable, and I feel as though I am picking up the pieces. When we started dating, it was light and we were not exclusive. We were both seeing other people. I told her I was going to see another girl for closure, and it ended up with her getting jealous and almost accusing me of lying. I had stated I would only be a couple of hours and I would be home early. It turned out to be the complete opposite as the encounter with the girl took far longer, and she tried to kiss me numerous times. I didn't give in and I ended up leaving the girl in amazement because of the rejection. I explained everything that happened to the girl I was dating, but her emotions took control and she said that she didn't want to ever speak to me again.

She explained her reaction the next morning and came clean about her distrust of men after what had happened to her. I met another girl a while ago and we dated for a while. Her ex-boyfriend used to beat her up and cheat on her, but then she would get a call from him and she would be gone. I couldn't understand it. I still don't. I would like to tell women like that, "Know your worth and don't settle for anything but the best." If you're in a relationship and you're not feeling appreciated, valued, or special, there is no point. Relationships are supposed to enhance your life, not beat you down.

My message to Mr Wrong would be, "Stop messing it up for us!" I've met so many women with trust issues and who have distorted views men. I've met women who say I'm too good to be true. They say they've never experienced anything like this. I've been with women who say they are just waiting to see what the trick is, when the other women will surface, or if I'm going to cheat. What you're doing here is destroying a woman's trust. You're making them insecure. I've dated women that think they aren't as pretty as I tell them. They don't wear certain clothes because they've been criticised by past partners. They don't accept compliments as they have never experienced them. Their self-esteem is so low. Crushing these things in a woman is a major crime. You create damaged good and we have to pick up the pieces. You should be building their trust and lifting their self-esteem, not crushing it.

Nathan, 31, London, England

No One is an Island

A successful relationship is based on trust and a willingness to be in it through an inherent desire to do the best by that person. Commitment is key. It means dedication and a willingness to do your best to create that longevity. Watching my parents' relationship break down has shaped the way I am in relationships. I have a great sense of wanting to do better where they have failed.

I've been cheated on. I dated someone briefly. She went to my school, and we bumped into each other by chance years later. She had a five-year-old, and she hadn't really got over the father of her child. He moved on, got married, and had more children with another woman. She told me that she had slept with him, and it hurt so bad, not just because I felt betrayed, but because I got on so well with her daughter. I felt bad because I could just imagine her asking where I was and knew that she would not understand why she couldn't see me anymore, which is exactly how I felt when my parents' marriage broke down and I didn't see my father anymore. She openly admitted that she had cheated on me and was remorseful and wanted to explain why, but when something like that happens, it's really hard to get the trust back.

I find some women paint men with the same brush—a very negative outlook—before the relationship even gets started. Guys almost have to be twice the man in her eyes just to be treated as a half-decent guy. If you put someone down long enough without good reason, they'll react. This is greatly unfair and very stressful state to be in. Unfortunately, the actions of a few bad men have ruined the situation for men that really are worth it.

I've been in that situation where I've been treated unfairly and with great suspicion to the point I even doubted myself.

On the flip side, some women need to look at themselves and the long list of 'I want this from Mr Right' and ask themselves, 'How much of this have I done for myself? Do I even measure up to the insanely high standards I expect from him?' Moreover, don't judge a man on where he is now. You as the woman may be the missing piece that inspires him to greatness, and a good man will always magnify and appreciate the works of a good woman in his life.

Men and Women need to stop, realise, and appreciate what each gender is about and their qualities in a relationship. I'm tired of people thinking they can do it on their own; nothing truly great is achieved alone.

Marvin, London, England

Damsel in Distress and Mr Prince Charming

The underlying topic that weaves these stories together is heartbreak. All the authors above have experienced heartbreak. As a result, some have become hardened, and others have simply repeated this heartbreak by breaking the hearts of women they form relationships with. How do we begin to deal with heartbreak and hurt, and does it differ across the genders?

Men are taught to be strong, to be tough, and to stand unfazed and undefeated in the face of adversity. From the dawn of time, men were given the role of hunters and gatherers, protectors and providers, and they were taught that the way to deal with problems is to fight it out in wars and duels. Fairy-tale stories teach us that women are 'damsels in distress' who wait as long as it takes for their prince or knight in shining armour to sweep them off their feet and rescue them from their loneliness.

Cinderella teaches young girls that we must suffer in order to gain happiness and that if we are good enough and wish hard enough, then we will get the man we deserve. And, of course, the man is rich and powerful, someone who can uplift their rescued damsel into a life of majestic bliss. Rapunzel relies on a passing prince to save her from her imprisonment, and 'fairer than fair' Snow White is rescued by another loved-up prince. These poor damsels in distress rely on these men to save them from the lives that have been inflicted on them through jealousy, hate, and bewitchment from evil witch-like characters. Furthermore, in a heart-beat they accept these men as their perfect husbands with no sense of discernment whatsoever. Fairytale stories have a lot to answer for!

The word 'damsel' comes from the French word demoiselle, meaning 'young lady', and the term 'damsel in distress' is a translation of the French demoiselle en détresse. It is an archaic term that can be traced back to the [2]knight errant found in medieval songs and folklore. Knight errants believed the saving of such women was an essential part of his raison d'être or 'reason of being.' Courtney talks about the demigod Perseus in The Clash of the Titans. His whole raison d'être was to court and marry the beautiful Princess Andromeda, daughter of King Cepheus, but not before a series of gruelling obstacles and challenges.

Through conditioning, men are taught to fight and win. You would never see a hero, warrior, or knight crying over a woman or 'talking it out' with his mates. He would never talk of his heartbreak to his warrior or knight friends whilst they listened intently over a hot cup of cocoa and passed him the tissues. No. He would win, and if he did not win, he would move onto the next quest with the wind in his hair.

So much of this has translated into modern society and the way gender roles are defined in relationships. As women, we tend to talk so much more about our feelings, our hurts, and our

---

2 a knight travelling in search of adventures in which to exhibit military skill, prowess, and generosity

pain and begin healing through the listening of and validation of our pain. In doing so, we can begin to learn valuable lessons, let go, and move on. The stories above reveal the underlying pain beneath the nonchalance and emotional disassociation the authors display as a means of protection within relationships. As women, we often forget the societal pressures placed on men in a patriarchal society where Mr Dreamer wants to be Prince Charming and Mr Ex Factor can't display or heal his hurt. Let's not forget though, ladies, we are no damsels in distress! Just as we have the power to heal, support, and nurture, we also have the power to protect, provide, and create. Just as men need the balance of both their masculine and feminine aspects, we do to. It's Ying and Yang baby!

Yes, there are many Mr Wrongs out there, but Mr Wrongs aren't born; they are made. Perhaps we can say Mr Wrongs are a creation of heartbreak, societal pressure to 'be a man,' lack of positive male role models, misrepresentation of women in the media, and worse still, as Marvin says, through some women's constant negative stereotypes or already low expectations of men. Above all though, perhaps Mr Wrongs are created through the lack of love and esteem they hold for themselves. Can a man who lies, cheats, and abuses women truly know his worth? As women we need to ensure we do not become the woman scorned. Nathan hits the nail on the head when he says, "Know your worth." If we can accept and love ourselves just the way we are, we should be able to accept compliments, expect men to treat us well, and believe we deserve better for ourselves than emotionally unavailable Mr Loose Eye or Mr Parasite.

In saying this, we need to live in the real world and realise that there are no 'knights in shining armour' or 'princes', just people, human beings who long to be loved and accepted too. We must not let our bitterness stop men from fulfilling their role as fathers no matter what our hurts may be. Sometimes we are not meant to be with every knight we have a relationship with, but when we do we have the power to breathe greatness into him and he, us. Sometimes our knights come wearing chipped armour or with a broken sword or even a broken heart. It is not our job to 'polish him up' or fix his heart but to stand alongside him as his Queen. What is ironic about these analogies is that when we both take off our armours and lay down our hurts and disappointments, we are Kings and Queens in our own right: of our hearts and our lives. What makes a relationship work is the realisation of this and the ability to gently remind the other of exactly who we are.

Chapter 13: Give Mr Right Some Love

In my quest to examine love and relationships, my own faith and belief in real love, although never died, has returned. I asked for inspirational relationship stories that celebrate and appreciate men who **are** providing and nurturing supportive, happy, secure, and loving relationships. There are men who pull their weight in a relationship; there are men who are not afraid of commitment, who follow through on their promises, and who make every effort to maintain supportive and loving relationships based on trust, honesty, respect, and of course, compromise.

Whilst Mr Wrong focuses on the lessons we can learn from unhealthy relationships with a man who is not right for us, this book is all about equality and celebrating the positive. This book is about inspiring women to believe that happiness, joy, and supportive and fulfilling relationships do truly exist. It's also about the fact that, with hard work, mutual respect, love, support, honesty, trust, understanding, kindness, and determination, love will prevail. Thank you, ladies, for sharing your stories.

Mr Supportive

Ryan and I met at work in England. I am from Australia and he is South African, so we were both far away from home. I was one of the people that interviewed him for his position. We noticed each other immediately, but it wasn't until the end of his contract that we ended up getting together. My initial reaction to him was that I thought he was good-looking but too conceited as he was hamming it up for the interview, but I soon changed my opinion when I got to know him.

- *What I noticed about him was:*

- *He was reliable and responsible. I knew he'd do something if I asked him, but he also knew how to have fun.*

- *He treated other women with respect.*

Most importantly, he wasn't ashamed of his mum. I remember once my colleague passed on a message to him in front of the 30-strong staff team that his mum had called and to call her back. His reaction was 'Oh, cool.' He was so happy to get the message and didn't try to act cool and dismiss her. I knew then that he was the man for me.

This was in 2006. We have been together since then, sharing the experiences of moving countries, having to be apart while visas were granted, and the wonderful joy of parenting our gorgeous son. We are more than a couple now; we are a team.

Last year Ryan and I suffered a loss. I was pregnant and the pregnancy was going very badly. I was in and out of hospital. One hospital visit ended up being the end of the road for the pregnancy. To save my life they had to remove the baby and I had to have an emergency hysterectomy. I also had a long recovery time both in hospital and at home.

This has really changed my life and my perception of myself and my future, and I have been struggling inwardly with everything— intimacy, depression, future aspirations, etc. My whole perception of myself was that I was going to be a mother of many, and now that has been taken away from me. Ryan was so supportive throughout all of this, through something that I believe would be the end of many relationships. Ryan has been patient, supportive, and strong throughout. He's been there for me when I needed time, counselling, space, and love (most of the time—he has his own demons from this ordeal that he has to work through too).

I now have body issues with scars on my stomach, excess skin, and extra weight from grief-eating, but Ryan never makes me feel like this is an issue or that it bothers him or that I am undesirable; furthermore, he is also supporting me in my weight loss journey.

I am happy to say that we are on the road to recovery together, that life is happy for us again, and we are looking forward. But it has taken time and I am thankful for him for being there for me and giving our relationship that time to come through this.

Hazel, 35, Australia

Mr Right after Mr Wrong

I met my husband through a mutual friend. There was a big group of us going into town and we were both invited. As I arrived late due to work, my friend introduced me to the people I didn't know, one of which was Dikkie. All his friends call him Eady, and that was how he was introduced, but because it was so loud in the club, I thought he said Stevie and that is what I called him for the rest of the night. Bless him—he didn't correct me!

The second I laid eyes on him I knew I had met someone special. I don't mean I knew I was going to marry him or that he was going to father my child or anything like that, but hand on thumping heart, I knew he was who I was waiting for. That sounds completely ridiculous, but I swear that's what happened! Suddenly, everywhere I went he was there! I never laid eyes on him before, but it turned out we drank in the same pubs, had many of the same friends, were at school together (different years), and went to the same college at the same time (but different courses although the departments are next door). We even worked in the same building together once! I worked at a wine bar when I was at college, and it was a new place and was still being fitted out. While I had my staff training, Dikkie was the one who fitted the bar there, and I actually remember sitting opposite the bar while it was being fitted. Small world!

This is exactly what I think about Mr Right being ready for you. If I had noticed Dikkie way back then, I doubt we would have lasted ten minutes. However, despite the universe clearly trying to throw us in each other's paths for years, we met when we both wanted the same thing. He is the first man who has never played mind games unlike the men in my experience. He was honest and straight up about everything, and I felt secure in the knowledge I didn't have to try to be anyone but myself to please him.

As for Mr Right, I don't believe everyone has a Mr Right. I think most people have a 'Mr Right Now' and that person is in their lives for a reason. As they grow and change, so do their needs and wants in their Mr Right. However, I do think some people are lucky enough that their Mr Right Now grows and changes with them and has the same needs as them (or at least can fulfil each other's needs) for their lifetime. I hope that's the case for me and my husband as he is one of the very few genuine, loving, and caring blokes I've ever met, and I would be gutted if he was my Mr Right Now instead! The reason I believe this is that I've had relationships with men that have not been 'the one' as such but have been perfect for me at the time we were together. Whether it ended badly or on good terms, I've still walked away with valuable lessons. Unfortunately, some relationships have left a bit of a sting and caused problems with future relationships, such as reduced self-esteem or just outright night terrors at one point (always a passion killer)!

I don't know what makes a relationship work in general, but I can tell you what makes ours work! We want the same things, we want to move in the same direction in life, and we want those things with each other. I guess it's like a work team as in we both have strengths and weaknesses and play to them. This works in the big and small things, e.g., I'm better with money so I deal with the finances (mostly—he always knows what's going on with it but I pay the bills, make the phone calls, etc.) and he is better with DIY so he does those kind of things. With the more important things in life, like making decisions, it is usually me that has the voice of reason; however, if something bad happens, then he is the rock for us all.

I think one of the most important things for us is that we try never to take each other for granted. This doesn't always work as life isn't that easy but we try! We ask each other every evening 'How was your day?' and it's not small talk. I genuinely want know how he has felt, has anything funny happened, is his boss still getting him down? Etc., etc. This helps me understand where his head is at on a grander scale. It means that he won't be bottling things up and end up more stressed than he needs to be.

I think making sure we are on the same page most of the time—or at least understanding which page each other is on if it's not the same—makes us chug along nicely. If we have different opinions, which in fairness is rare, then we compromise. Admittedly it is mostly me that gives in because Dikkie hardly ever asks anything of me, so when he does, I will bend over backwards to make sure I do it. He gives me free rein with most things and is happy that I'm happy.

When it comes to arguments, we are both rubbish at rowing and end up upsetting ourselves stupidly. We don't row very often, and if we do, it's never about anything important but it's usually horrible. He doesn't shout a lot but knows how to upset me; on the other hand, I'm a mouthy cow who turns into one of Jeremy Kyle's finest when I get mad. It's something we both try and work on, but it goes out the window when tantrums occur! I've been told many times that you should never sleep on a row and always make it up before bed, but we are terrible at doing that because we are stubborn. This leads me to stew a lot and think the worst of situations and even have a plan of action of what happens if we never make it up. It's the worst thing we can do and does damage for days. I hope time will help us fix this! I do believe if you have a great love for someone and don't want to hurt them, then you need to do the opposite to what we do!

I think making our home nice and taking pride in it works for us as well. We feel proud of what we have accomplished together and can relax more. 'Tidy room, tidy mind.' We are both terribly undomesticated but try very hard to make our little house a sanctuary for us and our daughter. She is our heart, and all we want is her safe and happy. For this to happen, we need a nice place to live!

We don't want or give many gifts as money is tight, but we make memories as a family and as a couple. In fact, that was our New Year's resolution this year—to make as many positive, happy memories as possible. Making good times and treasuring what's important is what makes our little world go round.

I know people come from all walks of life, but I feel that we have very similar backgrounds and our parents have instilled very similar morals and values into us. I believe this has made us stronger. For a start, we don't play mind games, ever! I don't believe in them and think it ends badly. They can start relationships based on lies as you are coming across to the other person as someone you are not and have gained their trust unfairly. Dikkie and I were up front and honest about what we wanted in life and hoped to gain from each other. We were lucky this was the same thing! I get that people shouldn't be too full on in a new relationship as it puts unnecessary pressure on it, but Dikkie told me straight up he was looking for a girlfriend not a fling. This allowed me to make the decision to go out with him instead of wondering what I was letting myself in for.

Jenna, 29, Rushden, Northamptonshire, England

Perseverance and Luck

At the age of 22 my parents advised me that I should start looking for a husband or else I would be left on the shelf. I was mortified; the biggest decision I made on a weekly basis at this stage of my life was where we would be drinking on a Friday night. I ignored their plea for about a year by crying every time they bordered the subject. When I turned 23 this strategy no longer worked. I had an option: either I find someone to marry or they would call on their friends and family for introductions. So that year I conceded. The search for a husband and 'Mr. Right' began!

I met some of the 'suitors' in coffee houses, pubs and even attended tea parties hosted by a match maker (parents included). Some men wanted a mother, some thought they would be my father; some clearly just didn't want to get married. There were accountants, bankers, doctors etc. but one thing I soon learnt was that the profession did not make the man. Well not for me anyway! The qualities that mattered to me were a kind heart and a sense of humour. I believed in romance, love at first sight and was waiting for my magical moment...there had to be a happy ending right? The search went on for about three years on and off, until my mum handed me a phone number which had promise.

We met in a pub. I was not swept off my feet as conversation was average and some of his views were not common to my way of thinking. We didn't share any interests but there was a flicker of a butterfly in my gut. We dated for a year and decided to get married. Looking back, although we cared for one another neither of us were 'in love'. I think we both knew we could potentially grow to love one another and were willing to take a gamble. The first year of marriage was miserable. I soon realised that until you live with a man you really don't know them. Inevitably we soon hit a cross roads; we had to dedicate ourselves to making this work or our marriage was best left in the past. I don't know what exactly triggered the next chapter of our relationship, but he stepped up.

I lost the vision of what I thought I wanted from a man. We had no expectations of one another and weren't consumed by images of what our 'roles' were. Today, ten years after our first meet, he is the father of my child, the love of my life and my best friend. We have grown to love and support each other. We did take a risk in getting married but who doesn't in every relationship? We both had a desire to make 'us' succeed and that's why he is my Mr Right!

Jyoti, 34, London, UK

The Conditions of Unconditional Love

In a few days my husband and I will celebrate our 24-year anniversary. For the most part it's been pretty easy. That isn't to say it hasn't been work. All relationships require work. Don't kid yourself into thinking they don't.

And don't think for a minute love is unconditional. No one should ever have to live in an unhappy, physically or emotionally abusive marriage to prove their undying love. There is a huge difference between being supportive, forgiving, patient, and encouraging and being turned into a used-up, tattered rag.

I'm lucky I found my husband. I'm lucky he became the man he is today. As a young girl, I would sometimes think of marriage and the kind of man I would have for a husband, but I never made a list of "must haves".

My husband and I were very young when we married. Like most young couples, we didn't put much thought into how much work marriage would be because we were in love. Older married couples would tell us how much work marriage was. Work? If you are in love, truly in love, a marriage is no effort at all, right?

Fast forward 24 years:

I have learned a lot. Overall, it has been easy—when compared with most marriages I've observed, it has been a real cake walk. It has also been a lot of compromise and sacrifice and WORK on both our parts.

In reflecting on my marriage, I decided to share a bit of insight about what has made my marriage work, and I hope that others may read and think about how they can make their marriages work as well.

Here are just a few things I thought of today:

Acknowledge each other

I get absorbed with my own personal agenda at times. I have the potential to become a bona fide workaholic, focused only on what I need to do and forgetting about the simple needs of others.

A few years ago, when our kids were very young, I was busily cleaning the house when my husband came home from work. I was mopping and barely looked up from the floor to greet him when he got home. I continued to clean while he took the kids to the park. When he came home, I was busy preparing dinner and probably carrying on with a few other chores as well. We went through the nightly routine of stories and baths and more cleaning. When we got into bed that night, my husband said, "You didn't even say hi to me when I came home".

Well, my first gut response to this was:

EXCUSE THE HELL OUT OF ME!! Are you not an adult? I do a million things all day long, so sorry I don't have time to acknowledge your presence when you walk in the door!

This is where marriage requires work. I could have easily blurted out my first thoughts. Then what? Hurt feelings, more hurtful words, grudges, and eventually resentment.

Instead, I apologized and asked him how his day was and told him about mine. In the end, it really wasn't so hard. Since then, I always make an effort to stop what I'm doing and say "Hi, what's up? How was your day? Guess what I did today?" But believe it or not, this is sometimes a real effort for me. It's not that I don't care about my husband; I just get preoccupied with other things.

Everyone deserves a little "me" time

My husband ALWAYS comes home after work. He never calls me to tell me he is going out with the guys—not that it would bother me if he did, especially now that the kids are grown. But I know men who do that all the time, and sometimes they don't bother to call at all. Then they wonder why their wives are so pissed when they come home at 1 a.m. with receipts for a $500 bar tab and glitter in their pants while she has been fighting homework battles and cleaning up puke. Once or twice a year? Cute, hope you had a good time, you are forgiven. Twice a week? You need to rethink your idea of "me" time.

There is nothing wrong with getting together with friends to cut loose a little. And there is nothing wrong with a spur of the moment call: "Hey, I'm gonna stop for a couple beers with Larry and Moe after work." But it isn't exactly fair to make a regular habit of this. Though it might hurt to tell your friends you need to get home—that is marriage.

I always found scheduled "me" time worked best, especially when there are small kids involved. It's far better to let the other person know you have plans to do something on Thursday night, so they can make their own plans too, and not spring it on them last minute. Not getting called at all? Well, we all know how that can end up.

You would call your boss to let them know you're going to be late or not be in at all. You would never expect your co-workers or your boss to put up with repeated tardiness or poor work performance. Why would you expect your spouse to put up with it?

You are no longer single

Regardless of your reason for getting married, you need to realize you are married, and there are certain things married people should not be doing. Coming home on a nightly basis at 1 a.m. with glitter in your pants is definitely one of those things.

The thing about money

Honestly, I cannot recall my husband and I ever fighting about money. We went through some financial difficulties, but we were always on the same page about how to fix it. Unfortunately, this is not the case in most marriages.

In our early years of marriage, we racked up a lot of credit card debt; we were young without kids, and we knew we were both equally to blame for the debt. After our son was born, we realized we had to get a grip on our spending. It took a lot of work, but together we got out of debt and managed to save enough money for a down payment on a house.

When most couples talk about cutting spending and saving more, I find they actually mean it's the other person who needs to cut and save. In some cases one partner may be more of a spender than the other, but in many cases I have found both partners have problems with spending. How often have you heard of spouses getting back at each other for spending money by going out and spending more money? One person splurges on a set of golf clubs, so to piss him or her off, the other person purchases a pair of $300 designer shoes. And it goes on and on, leading to more resentment, grudges, and debt.

As a side note: if you are fighting over who bought diapers last, you are really heading for trouble. Believe it or not, I actually heard a married couple arguing about this.

Show a little appreciation

There is no doubt in my mind that in most situations both spouses work hard. Sure, I know of a few situations where one person might not work outside the home NOR do they work inside the home—they are plain lazy. If you are currently depressed because you can't find a job, at least put yourself to work at home; there is always something that needs to be done. (On the other hand, if you have a serious issue with depression, please get help.) But in most cases both spouses, regardless of what their jobs are, work hard and deserve to be acknowledged for that.

Don't belittle your spouse because you think their job is so much easier than yours.

Don't make your spouse feel inadequate because you don't have the material things you want. Show more respect by being thankful for the things you have. Show appreciation for the things your spouse has provided or done for you. Take a look at what you have around you. Chances are you will find something you once loved and had to have and maybe worked very hard to attain—don't forget about that. Besides, if you want something bad enough, you most likely have the ability to go out and work for it yourself.

Accept that you may have to change

There are serious character flaws and personality disorders you will never be able to change in a person. Don't think for a minute you will change a philandering womanizer into a loving, caring, committed partner no matter how much he lies that you are "the one". You can also be sure that the gold-digging Barbie look-alike-wannabe will hit the road after she drains your bank account. Trying to change the other person will only lead to frustration, disappointment, and self-loathing.

Never, ever marry someone who displays any signs of having a poisonous personality disorder.

Instead of trying to change the other person, maybe you just might need to consider it is you who needs to change. You may need to be more giving, more flexible, less demanding. While changing who you are is not something that should be required to maintain a relationship, changing how you react and respond and communicate can be important in keeping a marriage together.

It is very easy to be the taker in a relationship. My husband is a giver. His giving sometimes gets on my nerves. He often goes without something to give me what I want. Why does this bother me? Because he deserves to have his wants met too—it isn't all about me. Doesn't sound like the attitude of a taker, does it? That's because I recognize I'm a taker and make a very conscious effort not to take but to give. Making a conscious effort is work.

Being an only child, I never had to learn how to share. Not that I didn't share—I never minded it at all—but at home my space was mine, my time was mine. I never had to compromise much because, for the most part, I was always alone. There wasn't anyone to talk to or who wanted to be talked to. It was easy to get lost in my own little world and worry only about my own needs.

I have learned a few things about myself in the last 24 years and why I am the way I am. I have worked hard to not let my natural inclination towards self-absorption leave my spouse feeling neglected or taken advantage of. More importantly, my husband has also learned why I am the way I am because I told him—I didn't make him guess, which is the first key to a good marriage: communication.

So, I think these are a few basic conditions of love: make an effort to pleasantly acknowledge the other person, include them in financial decisions, be appreciative of their efforts—no matter how small, give up your single life, and realize you are not the only one who needs a break every once in a while or that you are the only one with needs. All of this just comes down to one basic condition of love:

R-E-S-P-E-C-T

Of course, there could be many more conditions, and they will vary from person to person depending on one's tolerance and expectations, but hopefully these simple little acts of basic kindness will help you keep your marriage strong. It may require a bit of extra effort and work, but in the end all your hard work should be well worth it.

Marie Friddle, USA

If You Don't Ask, You Don't Get

It is evident from reading these positive testimonies that there are happy, healthy existing relationships based on mutual respect, honesty, and trust. It is also evident that, at times, these things need to be worked at. Everything worth keeping needs to be nurtured, cared for, and attended to. One of the key things in the above testimonies is the element of communication. Marie says in *The Conditions of Unconditional Love*, *"More importantly, my husband has also learned why I am the way I am because I told him—I didn't make him guess, which is key to a good marriage."* Although in this instance she is referring to being candid and frank about elements of her personality, in a broader sense, being honest and up front about what we want as well as who we are is also key. Asking.

We live in a society where asking for what we want is somehow forthright or self-centred. I grew up in a household where asking for things was wrong. "Ask and You Won't Get." This notion is not a new notion but one that perfectly mirrors society's values and collective belief. From one perspective, it can be seen as a positive thing: a child should be grateful for what they have and not seek to desire more. The idea behind it being that one should be satisfied and appreciative for what they have. However, there is a fundamental difference between never desiring for more and being appreciative for what we have.

I remember reading a children's story once about a little girl who kept on asking for more and more things from her tired mummy who ended up screaming, "You should be appreciative for what you have!" I remember puzzling over this: surely the little girl is appreciative that she has the God-given ability to ask? Whilst I don't agree that a child should be bought whatever they want simply because they have asked or shrieked over and over again for it, I do believe that we all have a fundamental right to ask for the things that we desire, require, need, or want without fear. This notion that we should not ask for things can be quite limiting and damaging as we start to file our needs, wants, and desires into the "unattainable dream" shelf and harbour resentment and unfulfilled desires.

"Ask and You Won't Get" is a notion that we are taught at home, in schools, and sometimes in the workplace. How many times have you feared to express that which you desire for fear of an all resounding, "NOOO!"? Yet this fear stops us from progression, stops us from grasping opportunities and unlocking doors to our rightful paths. Had we only asked, we may have received that pay rise, that promotion, that puppy in the window we so desperately wanted; we may have received that love we deserved. Although we may not always get what we ask for, asking allows us the opportunity to achieve our goals, create our happiness, and seek fulfilment.

As a child, I was lucky enough to have a mother who taught me about the world that extended beyond the world I knew. At eight I was fully versed on Apartheid in South Africa, Nelson Mandela, and starvation in Ethiopia. I remember, at the tender age of ten, watching and waiting to witness Nelson Mandela's first steps towards freedom. We all sat huddled around the television. It was a pivotal moment for me. I was dumbfounded when, at thirteen years old, other children did not know about Apartheid or the Holocaust. I was a very "sensitive child," as my teachers always described me in my primary years, and became very affected by the injustices and unfairness around the world.

When I was ten years old, my mother took us to watch a play called Sarafina featuring the exiled Miriam Makeba. Still to this day, watching that performance was one of the most profound moments of my life. It exposed me to a world of horror and injustice that was met with such strength, unity, and compassion. Again, I thank my mother for bringing this knowledge to me. My father, coming from a strong Jewish background and family, was able to impart knowledge through teaching me about the incredible and extraordinary journeys of my ancestors: journeys of pain and separation, loss and survival—the greatest pride being my great-uncle Salo, who, due to a missing signature on his passport, was unable to flea Germany and escape the terrible torture inflicted upon innocent people. He was tragically taken and experienced a variety of concentration camps, including Auschwitz, surviving only due to volunteering for every manual job the Nazis demanded. Those who did not have knowledge were shot, and those that did were kept alive. A real tale of wit and survival.

Having been exposed to these injustices early on and being taught on a daily basis to be grateful for what I have, I learned to never ask for anything as a child (or should I say, very rarely). It seemed unfair for me to whine for a Super Nintendo when others had so little. I carried around a huge amount of guilt. I remember waking up on my seventh birthday and seeing a pile of presents outside my door, waiting for my excited tiny fingers to unwrap them. Instead, not wanting to seem greedy or that all I cared about was presents, I stepped over them and went to the bathroom. I was just a little girl trying to figure out the rules of the world, and instead I appeared 'ungrateful.'

I became this way in relationships too, never asking for anything and expecting men to know what it was that I wanted and needed. Don't get me wrong—I would complain about what they **weren't** doing but not what I needed and wanted. Little did I know that not being honest about exactly what it is you need, want, and desire stops your man from feeling needed and sometimes wanted. Having broken up with a long-term boyfriend and having a heart-to-heart almost a year later, I clearly remember saying to him, "I never asked you for anything." His reply was simply, "Well, how can you complain about not getting something you didn't ask for in the first place?" For a moment I paused. He was right! If I asked for what I needed and wanted in the first place, I may have got just that! It is crucial for both the woman and the man to express what it is they need and want in a relationship. If you need a relationship based on honesty, say it. If you need a man who is reliable, voice it. Voicing your intentions speaks a message loud and clear about the things that are of value and importance to you. How we ask for the things we need and want is another question.

Asking for What We Want

Although we may feel at the end of our tether, do not let that Rottweiler within win. Don't feed it. Don't listen to it. Take a deep breath and voice your intentions firmly and lovingly. I've found flattery works well. Look at the two scenarios below.

Scenario 1

WOMAN: (answering her partner's call) You never call me when you say you will. It really pisses me off!

MAN: Err...

WOMAN: Don't you have anything to say for yourself? Can't you see that it hurts me?

MAN: (defensively) This is exactly why I don't ring you. You're always nagging!

Scenario 2

WOMAN: (answering her partner's call.) Hi babe, how are you?

MAN: (provides some reply about his day at work) I've had a really busy day at work. I'm sorry I didn't have time to ring you yesterday.

WOMAN: Thanks for ringing me today like you said you would. I feel good when you keep your word, and I love the chats we have. I was worried yesterday when I didn't hear from you.

MAN: (feels positive about himself) I'm sorry I didn't call you yesterday. I was held up at work till late, and by that time it was too late to ring you. I'll make sure to ring next time so you're not worrying.

WOMAN: I appreciate that.

As you can see, Scenario 2 is far more conducive to a positive, progressive relationship. The woman does not come across as angry and bitter like the woman in Scenario 1 but encouraging and genuine. Her initial response to the call shows **interest.** The question allows him to talk about his day and provides her with insight into what is going on in his life and world. She leaves him an opportunity to explain why he didn't call her the night before if he wishes.

She then thanks him for ringing as he said he would, making him feel **positive.** Men love a bit of praise as we found out in **Chapter 12: It's a Man's World.** She then couples this with explaining to him the direct impact his actions have on her, "I feel good when you...." Now, doesn't every man want to make their woman feel good? If not, he needs to get to steppin'!

Further praise and **positive reinforcement** is given to him about his conversational skills, making him feel praised and positive. "She loves chatting to me. Ah me dat![1]"

Her final sentence ends in her raising **concern** and worry. This makes him feel cared for and nurtured—a far cry from the yelling and accusatory tone of Woman 1. She then showed him appreciation for listening and for understanding what it was that she wanted in the future. Asking for what you want doesn't have to resort to the classic old "telling off" or "having a go." It can be realised by being direct about what you want in a positive way and making your partner aware of how their actions make you feel. The woman in Scenario 2 didn't have to outright say, "I want you to call me when you say you will" because she gave him an opportunity to explain himself before jumping down his

---

1 A patois expression. Exclamation "Check me out!"

throat. Asking for what you want can be realised in these four main steps:

- Interest – in his day, life, and world

- Positive Reinforcement – when he is getting things right

- Concern – when he is not

- Appreciation – when he listens and understands what it is that you want

I write this from the perspective of a woman who has jumped down a man's throat and jumped to conclusions before allowing for an explanation or even a "hello." I have never received a positive result nor a change in behaviour. I have also been the woman who has been yelled at for not doing this or that before having been given the chance to explain. I have never reacted positively to this or proceeded to provide the person with what they want; instead, I felt "nagged" and "vilified" and, as a result, rightly or wrongly or perhaps subconsciously, began to give them more of the same. When someone is yelling and screaming at us to live by their standards and do what they want, we feel unappreciated and manipulated and therefore less inclined to play ball. I know if I'm given the chance to explain or realise my actions have hurt another in a space of honesty, appreciation, and genuine desire to make a change for the better, I am more likely to take the other's feelings on board. When we are constantly focussing on what our partner is not doing and constantly berating them for it, we lose sight of what they are doing right. Focus on the positive, but be honest about what you want and the rest should fall into place.

So where did Woman 1 go wrong? Woman 1 was mad, bad, and angry before she even answered the call. The moment he dialled her number her man received nothing but anger and negativity from her. A turn on? No. Her rant left him stumped and befuddled as to how to respond. This kind of response could also be met with anger from the man who now feels defensive and accused. Remember, when we point the finger in anger, nine times out of ten, the finger will point right back at you. What could have been a decent discussion resulted in the man feeling self-righteous and justified in his actions. His "telling off" justified in his mind exactly why he doesn't follow through with his phone calls. "Why should I if all I'm gonna get is an earful!" I hear him mutter as he hangs up and slinks off to lick his wounds. Who wants their man ranting to friends and work colleagues about his "neurotic missus"?

Things to Remember for Asking for What You Want

- Asking for what you want doesn't make you needy. It makes you assertive and honest.

- Asking for what you want allows you to be honest with both your partner and, more importantly, yourself. If you don't know what your needs and wants are, why or how should he?

- Unfortunately, men are not psychic.

- Always be honest about what you want, whether it is a forthright "I need you to call me when you say you will," or whether you take a more subtle tone like the woman in Scenario 2.

- Never apologise for your needs and wants. You are entitled to have them.

- Just as you are entitled to have needs and wants, remember, your man isn't entitled to fulfil them.

- Whilst compromise is important for a balanced relationship, don't ever sacrifice your needs and wants completely. If you are unfulfilled, you cannot be happy. It is important for your partner to value the things that are important to you.

- Don't tell your man off. He is your equal, not a child. "Telling off" results only in resistance, and you may end up with more of what you don't want.

- Be thankful for all the positive aspects of your relationship and voice your appreciation.

- Focus on what he is 'getting right', not on what he isn't.

- Never dishonour yourself by keeping quiet about your needs, wants, and desires. You **are** important.

- Don't let that Rottweiler win!

Epilogue: Does Mr Wrong Really Exist?

There are so many fantastic men out there who can provide happy and healthy relationships. Throughout this book we have explored The Many Shades of Mr Wrong, The Power of Forgiveness, and shared our stories and experiences with "Mr Wrong" and negative relationships. Most importantly, in **Chapter 9: Why Are We Attracting These Men and Relationships?** we have also had a look at ourselves and our own shortcomings and set our intentions and expectations higher. If we, both men and women, got rid of our baggage and learnt to deal with challenges in a more positive and productive way, then perhaps we would all be right for each other! Interesting world? I don't think so.

We are all unique with our own set of interests, challenges, paths, and journeys experienced only by us and us alone. Life is an experience in which we can grow and change and learn, create and recreate. Through my experiences of toxic relationships and encounters with "Mr Wrong", I have grown stronger and wiser. Having said this, have they really ever been 'wrong' for me, or have they provided me with invaluable lessons I needed to learn at the time? To trust my intuition; to listen to that inner voice inside; to learn compassion, forgiveness, patience, and boundaries are but some of the lessons I've learnt and am still continuing to learn. For without my encounters with them, I would not have been able to write this book; to share, unite, and empower others. Is there such a thing as 'right' or 'wrong' or 'good' or 'bad' or is this all a learning experience that will gain us the strength to step away from all that is negative for us and set out on a positive path to all that draws happiness to us? There is no such thing as perfection. Just Love and Love, just as it is, is perfect.

As a secondary school teacher, I once asked my Year 9 class full of teenage boys, "What does love mean to you?" (I was teaching Romeo and Juliet at the time.) This 14-year-old boy stared back at me and said without hesitation, "Loving an imperfect person perfectly." He stopped me dead in my tracks. Yes! That's exactly what it is! Loving someone for all that they were, are, and will become. Loving them just as they are right now, without a wish or desire to change a thing about them because just as they are, they are perfectly designed to give and receive love in the best way that they know how without any intervention from you. They are perfectly equipped to deal with any challenge presented to them, not because you do it for them or that you try and "fix" them, but because they have you by their by their side for love, support, and guidance when needed.

Again loving somebody doesn't mean accepting their behaviour, and it is still important to have boundaries and let go of negative and toxic people and situations. Remember, the greatest love next to God, for those who believe, is the love you give to yourself. If your partner's flaws are more than "imperfections" and you feel you are being abused, put yourself first and walk away. You are a woman with purpose. You do not have to accept it. You should **not** accept it.

"Loving an imperfect person perfectly" means loving **yourself** just as you are. For how can we love another before loving ourselves? By accepting the imperfections of others, we begin to judge ourselves less harshly, to learn compassion and patience, and to also accept that we are indeed perfect in our own gloriously shining "imperfections." Only when we truly believe this will we reflect somebody who will love us romantically, unconditionally, and truly.

Real Love

real love is about respect,
not about keeping the other in check
love is inspiring the other to keep aspiring
keep evolving
together solving
real love doesn't exist in time, nor is it intricate
it's infinite
Simple and intimate
real love is about acceptance,
acceptance of all that was, is, and will be,
love isn't wrapped up and frilly
real love ain't got much time for ribbons and bows,
fancy lines and prose
It ain't about material shows
love cannot decrease
it only grows
real love is unconditional
regardless
facadeless
Real love doesn't come with terms and conditions
With booby traps and secret missions
Love works best when each other listens
love needs space to move and flourish
love needs love for it to nourish
love isn't fearful or insecure
love isn't addictive—needing more and more
real love is unconditional, everlasting, and true

love is for all, not for the few
real love is seeing my hair in the morning and not running a
mile
at the worst of his jokes, still raising a smile
encouraging them in the right direction
even if it means seeing less of them
real love doesn't judge, nor can it be measured
real love is permanent and should forever be treasured
love is respecting each other's individuality
real love isn't binding, love sets you free
real love doesn't diminish when they aren't 'who you want them
to be'
who you 'programmed' them to be
real love is the Power of honesty
real love has no expectations, only the Truth we see
Truth of the other in all their shining Glory
The Good, the Bad, the Ugly
.....
Love is to Truth as Simple is to Be.

Daniella Blechner 2006

Quiz Answers

Can You Spot a Serial Liar?

When a person is lying the evidence can usually be found in:

a) Type of words that are used

b) Non-verbal expression

c) Pitch and tone of voice

The addition of an epilogue when recounting events is a sign of:

a) A true story

b) A false story

c) Both

A person who is lying often recounts a story:

a)Starting from the end and ending with beginning

b) No sequential order

c) Using strict chronological order

A false smile uses:

a) All the muscles in the face

b) Only the muscle around the eyes

c) Only the muscles around the mouth

When recounting information liar will:

a) Use limited hand gestures

b) Over exaggerate hand gestures

c) Sit on their hands

When lying a liar will often touch:

a) Chest, arms, hands

b) Face, mouth, throat

c) Legs, feet and ankles

A common gesture for a liar is:

a) Interlocking hands behind their head

b) Scratching their nose or ear

c) Nodding incessantly

When liar's story will:

a) Contain lots of emotion

b) Lack emotion

c) Contain lots of detail

Liars commonly leave out words like:

a) Pronouns- I, me, my

b) Adjectives-describing words like beautiful, amazing, exhilarating

c) Adverbs- slowly, happily, excitedly

A real smile uses:

a) Lower half of face

b) The muscles around the mouth area

c) All the muscles in the face

Animators and Artists

Amde Anbessa-Ebanks

From getting orange squash and biscuit first for drawing He-Man, TMNT, and Thundercats, Amde knew he had a love of drawing and bring happiness and joy to people where ever he goes.

His first published work was for illustrating for a book called *Health and Nutrition, A Rastafari Perspective* by Kwemara Publications. He would go on to create comic book and CD album covers for artist Corey Johnson and a comic strip for T2R (Time 2 Rave) magazine. In late 2006, Amde and his uni classmate formed an animation and design studio called KSS (Kitchen Sync Studios) prior to this they were known as The CVA collective.

Amde animated for cartoon series called *Jet Boy* by Corey Davis as well the short film called *Hair We Are* written and directed by Daniella Blechner
Amde joined a group of beta testers for the drawing app game sequel Drawsomething2 and his work piece on *Games Of Thrones* was featured in The Huffington Post.

Amde is the illustrator for the Mr Wrong book and is currently creating his comic book series called *Swords and Guardians.*

www.amdecreations.carbonmade.com

Jason Lee

From an early age Jason Lee has always used his mind, body and soul to gain knowledge within the creative arts industry. At the tender age of 10, Jason wrote his book of poetry called *Sometimes You Feel Like Ice*, which was published to great acclaim, making him the youngest author on the Black Inks publication roster.

Since then, he has gone on to hone his skills in animation and storytelling by graduating from the Surrey Institute of Art and Design with a degree in Animation. This led to many work opportunities in animation and web design.

In 2004, Jason won his place on the Millennium Awards Fellowship (beating over a thousand others) to produce a historical website for ethnic minorities living in Great Britain. He was given the chance to train under the Skillset organization and offered employment with the BBC by working on the 1Xtra radio show.

In 2006 he was lucky enough to work full time as an animator for a television production company, picking up many skills along the way. This led to him launching the 'Jasonmation' company in 2013. It offers a wide range of content, which includes digital painting, graphic design, fine art, storyboards, wall murals, animation and video marketing, all to the clients' specific needs.

As Director of his own company, Jason continues to develop concepts and strategies for independent businesses and enjoys using his imagination when working within his chosen career of visual arts.

www.jasonmation.co.uk

Sunny Tellone

Sunny hails from United States and is the proud designer of the front cover of *Mr Wrong.* She is a freelance illustrator and toy designer who is best known for her creations at Tiny Robot Factory (www.tinyrobotfactory.com) and prop design on the popular children's series, *Lalaloopsy.* She attended Full Sail University where she received a Bachelor of Science in Digital Art and Design. She has illustrated and designed two children's books and is currently illustrating for animation. She has always been fascinated with animation and toys since she was little and loves that she gets to work in the field she feels passionate about.

www.sunnytellone.com.

Also by Daniella Blechner...

7 Shades of Love

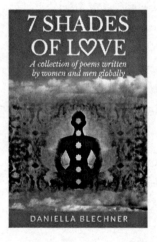

7 Shades of Love takes a unique approach to the ways in which various people, all poets, have dealt with Love.

Psychologists classify Love as an emotion; others deem it the highest of all universal frequencies. In a somewhat surprising correlation between the vital chakras of the human body and the ways in which we connect to and separate ourselves from love, Blechner illuminates how our energetic frequencies can influence our approach to love by a simple shift in balance. She's combined this with modern psychology and added the artistic writings of people from around the world in haiku, rhyme, and free verse.

Available in paperback, kindle and Epub

Special Dedications to

Francesca Blechner, Ron Blechner, Yvonne Blechner, Sue Patterson, Reg Patterson, Gareth Duffield, Vicky Crumley, Anthony Blechner, Renee Hirsch, Katie Blechner, Olivia Blechner, Naomi Kotler, Lawrence Coke, Natasha Cameron and Steve Botham, Nancy Wheeler, Anj, Sophia Bailey, Rachael Tirstatine, Amanda Epe, Mavreen Brown, Cezanne Poetess, Kuljinder Johal, Amde Anbessa-Ebanks, Shawn Peneloza, Charlie Innes, Leanne Moss, Melissa Gaynor, Millie Bavin, Chisenga Mala, Jacqui Weekes, Chris Warbarton, Matt Matthews, Daniel Fajemison-Duncan, Matthew Kinghan, Lauren Kirkman, Lola Atkins, Andre Farquharson, Laud Lartey, Ian Robert Sampson, Devron Callender, Segun Lee-French, Taru Khanna, Sarah King, Leah Noel, Cayman Grant, Seeds of Elevation, Ann Boswell, Adam Buck, Francesca Pritlove, DCosmic (Beyonder), Marlon Palmer and Moritz Formann

~For your kind support and faith in my project. ~

Mr Wrong, Daniella Blechner

294

Lightning Source UK Ltd.
Milton Keynes UK
UKOW05f0726200814

237182UK00001B/6/P

9 780992 991906